ARSENAL

ARSENAL

John Robertson

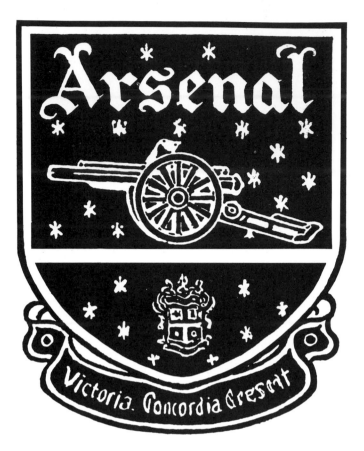

Endpapers *Tony Woodcock, bought to front Arsenal's attack for the Eighties*

Title page *Magic moments for Frank McLintock and the rest of the glorious Double winners at Wembley in 1971.*

Cover photograph *Kenny Sansom*

Contents

Published 1985 by
Hamlyn Publishing,
Bridge House, 69 London Road,
Twickenham, Middlesex.

Copyright © Hamlyn Publishing 1985
a division of The Hamlyn Publishing Group Limited

ISBN 0 600 50178 7

Printed in Italy

We're with the Woolwich!

Top *Fred Beardsley, the former Nottingham Forest player who became Arsenal's first goalkeeper.*

Above *Joe Powell, captain for the club's League debut.*

Preceding pages *The entrance to the old Woolwich Arsenal, now a Ministry of Defence building. Note the cannons on either side of the clock tower.*

In an area of the Isle of Dogs now almost certainly occupied by a housing estate or a huge office complex, there was once a small strip of derelict land that served as the pitch for an historic football match. It was bounded by back gardens with an open sewer running across one end. There, one day towards the end of the last century, a ragtag and bobtail assortment of players turned out for their first competitive game. They'd clubbed together to raise the grand sum of 52½p to get started and their kit comprised a mixture of odd-coloured shirts, odd shorts and knickerbockers, and shinpads worn outside their socks. They looked a motley crew, but there was no denying their skill with the soccer ball, for they beat the Eastern Wanderers 6–0.

In those days they called themselves Dial Square. Today they're the mighty Arsenal!

The year was 1886 and the seeds of the Gunners' rise to fame were sown in the workshops of the great Woolwich armaments factory, the Royal Arsenal. Soccer, or Association Football, was hardly known in the area, where Rugby was the name of the game. But when migrant workers moved down in search of work from the Midlands, the North and Scotland, they brought their soccer tradition with them. They took jobs at the ordnance factory as engineers and mechanics and soon founded the Dial Square club, which was named after one of the workshops.

After that first match they set about organising some proper kit. Red was chosen because some of the players came from Nottingham, where they had been members of the famous Forest club, and had brought their red shirts with them. Indeed it was Forest, founded some 20 years earlier in 1865, who supplied the club with their first set of shirts, after a request from one of their ex-players. Next came a change in name, from Dial Square to Royal Arsenal, so that the club had a wider identity. Home games were played on Plumstead Common and their first season's results read: Played 10, won 7, drawn 1, lost 2. Goals for, 36; against 8.

Their keenest local rivals were the Millwall Dockers, whom they beat 3–0 in their first meeting. Although they were obliged to move pitches from time to time, the Woolwich Reds, as they were known, began to attract quite a reputation. One of their members, Fred Beardsley, had kept goal for Nottingham Forest in the FA Cup.

Early facilities were very limited, with the team changing in a local pub and a 'grandstand' consisting of military wagons borrowed for the occasion. It wasn't until they bought one of their former grounds, the Manor Field in Manor Road, that they were able to build a stadium worthy of the name. By this time Royal Arsenal had become so successful – they were already proclaimed Football Champions of the South – that they had decided to turn professional and changed their name to Woolwich Arsenal. The year was 1891 and the decision was a bold step forward for a club which had been in existence for only five years. Although Arsenal had won all the London cup competitions and had overtaken clubs such as Tottenham Hotspur and Millwall, who had been formed before them, as amateurs they were unable to compete with the big clubs of the North. This was brought home to them by an FA Cup match in which they played the Swifts, one of the leading sides in the country, and were beaten 5–1. But there was a stigma attached to professionalism in the south and this was to threaten the very existence of the club over the following years. Nevertheless, inspired by the club's development and its huge following – it was drawing crowds of up to 12,000 – the move was taken.

The first result was that the club was excommunicated by the London FA. Most southern clubs, who were still amateur, cancelled their fixtures with them. The Woolwichers were forced to travel long journeys to the Midlands and North to find fixtures and their home support dwindled. They tried to persuade Southern clubs such as Spurs, QPR, Millwall and Fulham to join them in a southern league but when this idea was rejected, Arsenal took their next major step: they applied for membership of the expanding Football League. In 1893, they were admitted to the Second Division and set out on a League career which was to lead them to unrivalled supremacy some 40 years later. Arsenal owe their origins and survival through their early troubles to men like David Danskin, the founder member who instigated that first whip-round to buy a match ball, and John Humble, who led the march to professionalism and become chairman of the club.

Their early League progress was moderate. Playing back at the Manor Ground, which had been transformed for their debut by an army of enthusiastic supporters, they proved hard to beat. But with long journeys made all the more tiring by poor transport, their away form suffered. Arsenal finished 9th in their first season and continued their mid-table position for the next few years.

Arsenal's first captain in the League was right back Joe Powell, a powerfully built man whose play typified the rugged and physical style of the day. Like several other players during the Woolwich years, he'd been bought out of the Army. Scots were also sought for their skills and at one time they held eight of the 11 places.

Despite the club's entry into the League, it was still poorly supported and therefore couldn't afford to keep star players. Men like Caesar Llewellyn Jenkyns, a Welshman who was Arsenal's first international cap and captained the club in 1895–96, left for richer pastures and at one stage, in 1897, the club slipped back to 10th in the Second Division. The fan troubles which beset today's game were also in evidence even then, and the Manor Field Ground was closed for six weeks following an assault on a referee.

The Royal Arsenal team of 1888, captained by Arthur Brown pictured on the left of the three seated players.

Plumstead Common today...a century ago it was the stage for the first act of a football phenomenon.

Opposite *Caesar Llewellyn Jenkyns, Arsenal's first international. For some of their early games the club played in stripes of red and pale blue.*

The appointment of its first professional manager reversed the decline and by the turn of the century the club's performance was showing a steady improvement. Although overshadowed by Tottenham, who won the FA Cup in 1901 while still in the Southern League – which was formed the year after Arsenal's original proposal had been rejected – the club saw its efforts rewarded in 1904. After a close race with Preston and Manchester United for the Second Division title, Arsenal finished second behind Preston and gained promotion. The man who largely made it possible was Harry Bradshaw, who had been appointed manager at the turn of the century. He inherited a fine Scottish defender called John Dick and with a combination of shrewd local recruitment and some inspired fund-raising – an archery tournament raised £1200 – Arsenal quickly pulled out of their decline. Their captain was another Scot named Jimmy Jackson, who played at left back and was noted for his tactical ability. In their promotion season Tommy Shanks was leading scorer with 25 goals as Arsenal amassed 91 for and only 22 against.

Arsenal made their First Division debut under new management. Bradshaw was tempted by a big offer from Fulham and the new man at the helm was Phil Kelso, a tough Scot who twice guided them to the semi-finals of the FA Cup. League performances were average, but backed by some big crowds the club was able to buy some outstanding players. There was centre forward Bert Freeman, outside right Bill Garbutt, England international Tim Coleman at inside right and left back Jimmy Sharp, who was bought from Fulham to replace Jimmy Jackson.

Kelso's best season was 1906–7 when Arsenal finished seventh in the League

and reached the semi-finals of the Cup for the second successive year. But then they went into a tail-spin from which they were lucky to survive. Clubs like Tottenham and Chelsea were now in the League and easier to get to than Plumstead. As Arsenal's form faltered, their supporters drifted away. Kelso left for Fulham and there was no money to buy star attractions. In 1909-10, Arsenal escaped relegation by only two points and their financial situation was grave.

It was at this point that they were rescued by Henry Norris, the chairman of Fulham. He wanted to take over the club and move it to Craven Cottage. Norris, later to become an M.P. and to receive a knighthood, was a ruthless and determined man. He was also rich and influential. Although his proposal to amalgamate the two clubs was rejected by the League, Norris set about restoring Arsenal's fortunes in a way that the League felt powerless to challenge.

But matters were to get considerably worse before they got better. Although Arsenal tried to boost support by signing players like Alf Common, who commanded soccer's first £1,000 transfer fee when he moved from Sunderland to Middlesbrough in 1905, they continued to lose matches. They were once again forced to sell to survive and among their worst losses was wing-half Andy Ducat, who had been bought from Southend by Kelso. He was the first of a long line of international cricketer-footballers who have played for Arsenal and in addition to winning six England soccer caps, he scored 52 centuries for Surrey and made a Test appearance against the Australians in 1921.

In 1912, the inevitable happened. Arsenal won only three games and finished bottom of the First Division with 18 points from 38 matches. With Division Two soccer only a matter of months away, Norris had to move quickly. New sites were sought but none south of the river materialised. Then came the possibility of leasing land used by St John's College of Divinity at Highbury. Norris negotiated a 21-year lease at a cost of £20,000, the only proviso being that the club could not stage games on Good Friday and Christmas Day. (When the club later bought the site outright, this was rescinded). Arsenal now had a ground only 12 minutes by Underground train from the centre of London. Although there were protests from Tottenham, Chelsea and Clapton (later Leyton) Orient, the League accepted the move because there was no rule to stop it.

Thousands of fans packed the old Manor Ground to see the Woolwichers in action.

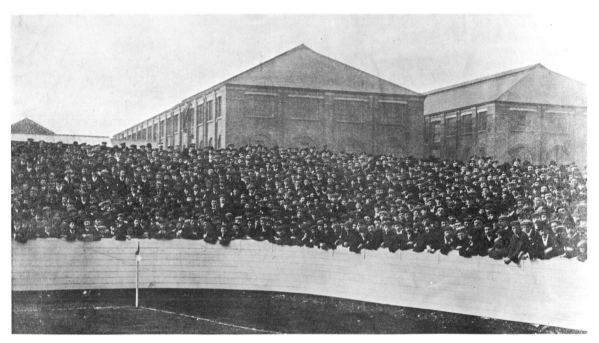

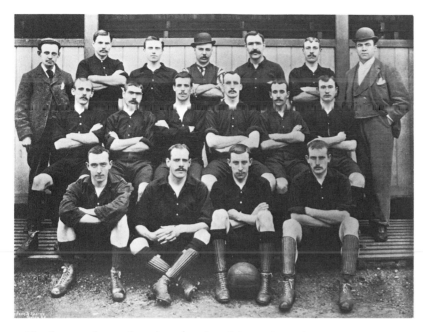

The Arsenal squad of 1895–96.

The League also made it clear that they felt North London was big enough to support both Arsenal and Spurs. With this coup accomplished, the ambitious Norris paused only to draw breath before playing his next ace. Facilities were limited in the early days while stands were built and the pitch levelled (it had to be raised 11 feet at one end and lowered five feet at the other to neutralise the slope of the area between the top of Avenell Road and Gillespie Road.) Norris also dropped the name Woolwich at this point and the club were known as The Arsenal. Having played their last game at Plumstead in April, 1913, they began the new season at Highbury with a 2–1 win over Leicester Fosse the following September. Among the team that day was another cricketer-footballer, Wally Hardinge. Unlike Ducat, he never played soccer at international level but coincidentally won a Test cap against the Australians in the same year. Arsenal finished the season in a nailbiting race for promotion with Bradford Park Avenue. Notts County were the runaway leaders; Bradford shaded Arsenal for

19

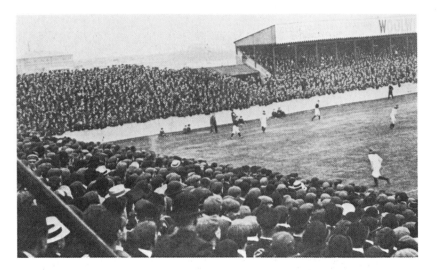

The opening game of the 1905–6 season against Liverpool (white shirts) at the Manor Ground.

second position on goal average. Norris had spent more than £100,000 on moving and improving the club and when the Great War began in 1914, there was little chance of the club being able to pay its way, let alone repay its debts. Arsenal finished the 1914–15 season in fifth position and League soccer was replaced by the London Combination.

In 1919, Norris pulled his most audacious stroke. The War over, the League had decided to expand each Division by an extra two clubs to a total of 22. Norris knew that for Arsenal to survive their deepening financial crisis, they had to get back into the First Division. By now Sir Henry Norris M.P., he used his position and influence to the greatest degree in canvassing support for Arsenal's restoration. He drew attention to Arsenal's length of service and loyalty to the League and brilliantly outflanked neighbours and rivals Spurs, who were hoping for and expecting a reprieve despite having finished bottom of the First Division in 1915. By managing to get their re-election discussed as a separate matter from that of Chelsea, who had finished second from bottom, Norris was able to divide and rule.

Derby and Preston, the two top teams in Division Two in 1915, were elected along with Chelsea and then came the crucial vote on whether it should be Arsenal or Spurs who joined them. Norris had won the key backing of the League president, John McKenna, and it was McKenna's eloquent speech which carried the day at the annual meeting. Arsenal were elected in with 18 votes to Spurs' eight.

Norris had already appointed Leslie Knighton, formerly with Huddersfield and Manchester City, as manager and so in every sense Arsenal were given a fresh start for the reopening of League soccer for the 1919–20 season. But there were constraints. With debts of around £60,000, Norris imposed a transfer limit of £1,000. Knighton had inherited some good players in men like Joe Shaw and Jock Rutherford and he strengthened the side with the addition of two outstanding amateurs, Reg Boreham and Dr Jimmy Paterson. Arsenal finished their first season in 10th position and with the odd hiccup continued their mid-table performance for the next few seasons. However by the end of 1924 it was clear that Arsenal's situation was once more in decline. Knighton tried his best in difficult circumstances and in one celebrated instance, against West Ham in the FA Cup, even resorted, in vain as it turned out, to the use of pep pills! By the end of the 1924–25 season, Arsenal had slipped perilously close to relegation, finishing 20th.

Far from fulfilling Norris's objective of being the best club in the country,

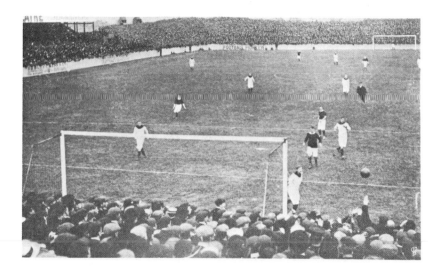

Arsenal were looked on as one of the poor relations of the First Division; a soft touch. Norris sacked Knighton and advertised for a manager with the caveat: 'Anyone thinking of spending large sums of money on transfers need not apply.' At Huddersfield, a man called Herbert Chapman was just completing the second leg of the club's historic hat-trick of three successive League championships.

One of the last games at the Manor Ground, in 1913.

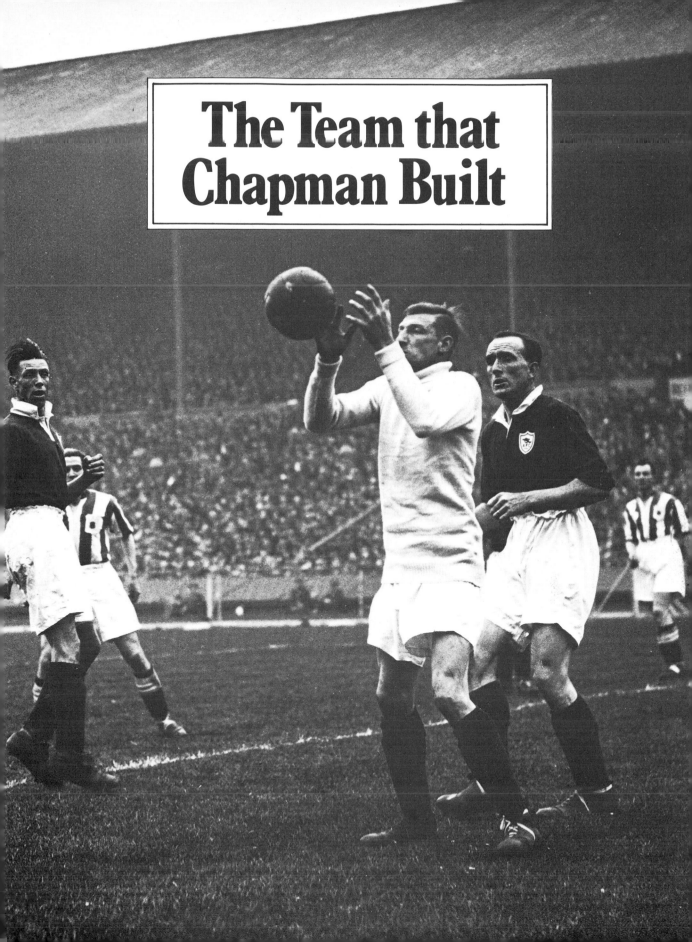

The Team that Chapman Built

The bust of Herbert Chapman which stands in Highbury's marble entrance hall.

ARSENAL owe their stature as one of the world's most renowned football clubs to the man whose bronze bust stands in the famous marble entrance hall of Highbury. That man was Herbert Chapman, a visionary whose powers created the greatest team and the greatest club soccer had ever seen.

There was nothing which marked out the young Chapman as a man of destiny. He was the son of a Yorkshire miner and showed more promise as an engineering student than in soccer, which he played for some ten years as a sturdy wing half around the turn of the century. What was special about Chapman was that he had a vision of greatness and an unswerving faith in his ability to realise it. He was an immensely energetic man with a flair for business, an eye for detail and a persuasive way with words. But above these qualities, he was able to make all those that worked with him believe in his dream. He once told his trainer, Tom Whittaker, who was later to follow in his footsteps 'Tom, I'm going to build the greatest club in the world.' He meant it and he did.

It was Chapman who brought the great Charlie Buchan to Highbury, it was Chapman who signed Alex James and the host of other names who became legends in their own lifetime; it was Chapman who changed the name of the local Underground station to Arsenal; it was Chapman who updated Arsenal's kit to the famous red shirts and white sleeves; and it was Chapman who launched them to five League titles and two FA Cup wins in a blaze of success unequalled before and only surpassed by Liverpool since. Sir Henry Norris must take some of the credit, for it was his ambition to make Arsenal a power in the land and it was his masterstroke in appointing Chapman. But Chapman was the architect and inspiration of all and more than Norris dreamed of.

Chapman was born in the mining village of Kiveton Park in West Yorkshire on January 19, 1878. Between 1897 and 1907 he played for various clubs almost at the rate of one a year, finishing the 1906–7 season with Tottenham, who were then still in the Southern League. His one distinguishing characteristic, apart from his tubby build, was that he wore bright yellow boots. In 1907 he moved on to become player-manager of Northampton, where he showed his organising ability by leading them to the Southern League championship in just two seasons.

The onset of the First World War found him back in Yorkshire, appropriately in view of his future career with the Gunners, in charge of a munitions factory. He maintained his soccer connections by managing Leeds City during this period. However when financial irregularities came to light, he was suspended along with club directors. It could have been a fatal blow to his career but Chapman was later cleared and the suspension lifted. In 1920 he joined Huddersfield as assistant manager and within a month had taken over the top job.

Huddersfield won their first ever league championship three years later in 1924, their second the following season, and by the time they were completing their then unique hat-trick in 1926, Chapman was already planning a glorious encore at a club 200 miles south. His achievements had so impressed Norris that he made him an offer he couldn't refuse…£2,000 a year to become manager at Highbury. For his part, Chapman saw in Arsenal the scope to create success on a far bigger scale than was possible at almost any other club in the country. Arsenal were down on their luck but perfectly placed, near the centre of the capital, to win massive support and acclaim if he could turn the tide.

Though Chapman would make no promises of instant success – indeed he forecast it would take five years for the club to win their first major honour – he quickly set about realising his ambitions. One of his first and shrewdest moves was to appoint Tom Whittaker, a former player, as trainer. Chapman recognised the value of physiotherapy at a time when this aspect of the game was receiving little attention. Keeping his players fit, and getting his injured players back in the game sooner than had previously been possible, were to be key factors in

Opposite *Herbert Chapman, a football visionary.*

Preceding pages *Arsenal goalkeeper Preedy stops a Huddersfield attack during the 1930 Cup Final.*

Arsenal's success. Chapman set about making Whittaker and Highbury examples of excellence in this field. Whittaker was sent to study the subject under a distinguished surgeon while Chapman equipped Highbury with the best and latest medical and training facilities.

Norris had been impressed by Chapman's ability to manage on meagre resources at Huddersfield, and because of Arsenal's financial situation he made it clear that he expected Chapman to do the same at Highbury.

However a combination of Chapman's persuasiveness and Norris's need for a crowning glory to his distinguished career soon changed all that. Chapman convinced Norris that he had to spend to succeed and and set about buying the best players that money could buy. Arsenal soon became known as the Bank of England club. It didn't matter that Chapman's own knowledge of the game was at that stage limited. Any weakness in matters of tactics would be more than compensated for by the strength of the men he bought. He instituted regular talks with his players to discuss how the battles could be won and so there developed a Team Chapman.

His first major purchase showed the new Arsenal management's flair for business and publicity. Charlie Buchan had once been an Arsenal player at Woolwich but had left in disgust when a former manager rejected an expenses claim for 11 shillings (55p). It was Arsenal's loss. Buchan went to Sunderland where he became a prolific goal-scorer, winning a championship medal in 1913, a loser's FA Cup medal the same year and international honours with England. Buchan was 34 by the time he played for Arsenal but on Sunderland's insistence that he was still capable of scoring 20 goals a season, Norris struck a deal which was to be the forerunner of many a future transfer. He agreed a fee of £2,000 plus £100 for every goal Buchan scored in his first season. With the offside law changed that year, reducing from three to two the number of players required to be between the goal and an opposing forward to keep him onside, Buchan's task was eased. With the goals beginning to flow again after a period of stagnation, he scored 19 times in the League and twice in the Cup. Arsenal finished a highest-ever second that season behind Huddersfield, who completed their record third consecutive success.

Chapman benefited from Buchan's immense knowledge of the game. Indeed it was Buchan who showed him the possibilities opened up by the new offside

The nightmare moment Dan Lewis let the Cup slip for Arsenal in the 1927 Cup Final.

law and thus laid the foundations for an Arsenal style which was to become known as the 'W' formation. The seeds were sown after a disastrous start to that first season in which the Gunners were thrashed 7-0 by Newcastle. Buchan, who had been appointed Arsenal captain, persuaded Chapman that because teams were now able to push more players into attack, their opponents needed more cover at the back. Buchan argued that instead of the centre half joining up with the attack, he should stay back and play as a third defender between the full-backs. Other teams were already adopting this style of play and Chapman agreed to the suggestion but insisted it would require one of the inside forwards dropping back to act as a link between attack and defence. Since he didn't want to lose Buchan's sharpness in front of goal, the choice for link man went to a young reserve called Andy Neil – 'slow as a funeral but clever on the ball' said Buchan – while Jack Butler (and later the great Herbie Roberts) became third back. The effect was immediate. Arsenal tried it out in their next match, at West Ham, and won 4–0. They never looked back.

The following season they made their first ever FA Cup Final appearance after hard-won victories over Liverpool, Wolves and Southampton. Their opponents at Wembley were Cardiff City, a mid-table First Division side whose basic plan was to mark Buchan out of the game. It worked and with 15 minutes to go and the score goalless, Arsenal's Welsh international goalkeeper Dan Lewis made an error which haunted him for the rest of his life. Going down to cover an apparently harmless shot by Cardiff centre forward Hugh Ferguson, Lewis fumbled the ball and watched in horror as it trickled over the line. Cardiff won 1–0 and the Cup left England for the first and only time in its history. Lewis was so upset that he tossed his loser's medal on to the Wembley turf and it was left to his team-mates to go and recover it. Arsenal finished 11th that season and in October, 1927, Chapman made the next move in his reconstruction by signing another of the players to become a Highbury hero. This was a young left back from Kettering Town called Eddie Hapgood.

Chapman paid a mere £950 and Hapgood made it one of his best bargains by becoming a magnificent defensive pillar over the next decade. Arsenal finished the 1927–28 season in mid-table and reached the semi-finals of the Cup where they went out to the eventual winners, Blackburn Rovers. The end of that season was a critical period in Chapman's development programme. Charlie Buchan

*A narrow escape for Cardiff as
Arsenal players Buchan, Blyth and
Brain (dark shirts) press home in the
1927 Cup Final.*

retired to go into journalism and in the course of the next 12 months, Chapman bought the trio of players who were to complete the jigsaw. In October, 1928, he set a British record transfer fee of £10,890 for Bolton's inside right, David Jack, the man who scored the first ever goal in a Wembley Cup Final (for Bolton against West Ham in 1923). Alex James followed from Preston for £9,000 in the close season and so too did Cliff Bastin, picked up for a snip from Exeter City. Bastin was only 17 and became known as Boy Bastin, a brilliant outside left. Before he was even 21, he had won every major honour – the League championship and FA Cup with Arsenal and International caps for England.

Arsenal, meanwhile, had an indifferent 1928–29 season, finishing ninth in the First Division and going out of the Cup in the quarter-finals. The arrival of Scotland international James at inside left and Bastin at outside left soon made its impact. Arsenal now had a solid defence built around their great stopper centre half, Herbie Roberts, and a forward line which developed into the regular combination of Joe Hulme (who also played cricket for Middlesex), David Jack, Jack Lambert, Alex James and Cliff Bastin. Early results in the 1929–30 showed no indication of the success that was about to swamp the club over the next decade. As the chance of the League title slipped away, Arsenal channelled all their energy into the Cup. It was Chapman's fifth season at Highbury and he had spent more than £30,000 in assembling a side which still didn't seem to click. After victories over Chelsea, Birmingham, Middlesbrough and West Ham, Arsenal found themselves up against lowly Second Division side Hull City in the semi-finals. A shock looked likely when Hull built up a 2–0 lead, but the day was saved by Bastin who hit a late equaliser and Arsenal won a bruising replay 1–0.

In their second Cup Final in four seasons, Arsenal lined up against Huddersfield. James made the vital early breakthrough amid protests from Huddersfield. Taking a quick free kick on the nod rather than the whistle of the referee, he received a return pass from Bastin and hammered the ball into the net. Having dropped back to accommodate Chapman's policy of employing him as the midfield link, James had turned from goal-taker to goal-maker during the season and his Wembley effort was one of only a handful that year. Lambert added a second for Arsenal, who captured the first of their glittering prizes with a 2–0 win.

Success bred success. The following season Arsenal won the League title for the first time with a record-breaking 66 points, a total not passed until 1969 when Leeds totalled 67 (this was under the old two-points-for-a-win system). The side which was now establishing itself as 'the team that Chapman built' read: Scottish international Bill Harper in goal (alternating with Dutchman Gerry Keyser and Charlie Preedy), right back and skipper Tom Parker, left back Hapgood, centre half Roberts, left half Bob John, Bill Seddon and Charlie Jones sharing the right half berth, and a constant forward line of Hulme, Jack, Lambert, James and Bastin.

The cup win over Huddersfield started a sensational run of success leading up to the Second World War:

1930: FA Cup winners
1931: League champions
1932: Cup runners'-up, second in league
1933: League champions
1934: League champions
1935: League champions
1936: Cup winners
1938: League champions

A vital moment in Arsenal's history as Alex James' shot puts the Gunners 1–0 up in the 1930 Cup Final against Huddersfield, the club's first major triumph.

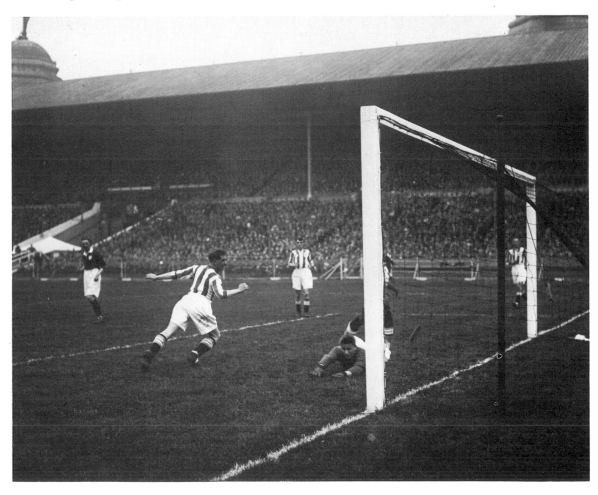

Glory at last...the victorious 1930 Cup-winners (from left) Preedy, Parker, Seddon, Hulme and Lambert.

In that first championship-winning season, Arsenal also broke the First Division scoring record by more than 20 goals, reaching a formidable total of 127.

In 1931–32, Arsenal came the closest yet to completing the first League and Cup Double of the century. But in a dramatic finish to the season, they were denied both honours. Everton shaded them for the League title by two points and Newcastle beat them at Wembley in the famous 'over the line' final.

Arsenal, whose route to Wembley had included an 11–1 win over non-League Darwen, were hampered by the loss through injury of James. Chapman moved Bastin to inside left and Bob John to outside left, bringing in young George Male at left half in his first Cup match for the Club. Male had been signed from non-league Clapton only that season and was another Chapman player destined for the Highbury Hall of Fame.

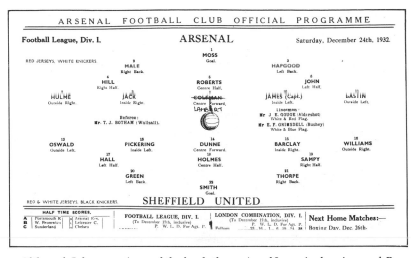

The line-up for the League game against Sheffield United which Arsenal won 8–2 on Christmas Eve, 1932. A few days later they lost to Walsall in the Cup.

Although John gave Arsenal the lead, they missed James' scheming and Bastin's raids. Five minutes from half-time came Newcastle's controversial equaliser. A long ball down the right appeared certain to go out of play, or so it seemed to Arsenal players as they pulled up expecting a goal kick. But Newcastle's inside right, Jimmy Richardson, continued his chase and crossed for Jack Allen to put the ball in the back of the net. Despite Arsenal's vigorous protests and to the disbelief of many fans, the referee allowed the goal to stand. Allen went on to score again and Newcastle's 2–1 win set them up as Arsenal's Cup Final bogey team. Twenty years later they would once again spoil Arsenal's Wembley day.

The 1932–33 season proved in many respects to be one of the most historic in the annals of Arsenal. It was the first leg of their championship treble, the season in which a new 21,000-capacity West stand was opened, the season when Chapman brought in the new white-sleeved shirts, and the season Chapman changed the name of the old Gillespie Road Underground station to Arsenal. It was also, of course, the season of Walsall.

Few defeats have ever gained so much newspaper prominence as the day Arsenal came a cropper in the mud at Fellows Park. It was the third round of the Cup in January, 1933. Victory over a side more than 50 places below them was almost taken for granted at a time when the Arsenal machine was running into top gear. Chapman 'rested' three internationals, Hapgood, John and Lambert, who were said to be ill or injured, left out Hulme, who was off form, and named a side which included three youngsters making their senior debuts. Atrocious playing conditions reduced the match to a lottery. If any one factor looked like tipping the scales, it was the heart for a battle. Walsall tore into their opponents from the start. Arsenal stars like Alex James were thrown off their game and Walsall finally converted their courage and determination into goals.

They scored twice in the second half to send the Gunners to their most famous defeat. The 2–0 scoreline is said to have prompted some incredulous newspapers to double check with their reporters in case they got it the wrong way round. Whether Chapman underestimated the task or whether his side was genuinely affected by illness and injury will never be known. The club certainly didn't let defeat hinder their League progress where they clinched the title by four points from Aston Villa and amassed 118 goals, including a 7–1 win at Wolves. Cliff Bastin set a record for a winger with a total of 33 goals – a mark which stands today and probably for all time. The hallmark of the Arsenal smash-and-grab style in those days was a punt upfield by the goalkeeper, a pinpoint first time pass from James out to Hulme on the right wing and a cross from

The plaque at Highbury commemorating the three successive League championship wins in the Thirties. Below is a bust of former club chairman Denis Hill-Wood.

Hulme which Bastin would meet with his left foot as he powered in towards the far post. Although Chapman's men had earned the familiar tag 'Lucky Arsenal' for a succession of home Cup draws in previous seasons, plus a reputation for snatching 1–0 wins against the run of play, the sheer volume of goals they scored during the Thirties gave the lie to the epithet.

With two League titles under their belt, Arsenal were on their way to another when tragedy struck in the New Year of 1934. Chapman, who had once told his trainer, Tom Whittaker, that to succeed you had to work 25 hours a day, fell victim to his own devotion to duty. He was already run down and suffering a heavy cold when he insisted, against doctor's advice, on spending a bitterly cold January evening checking out another player. He caught a chill and within a couple of days he died. The suddenness of Chapman's passing stunned not only the club but the whole of football. He was only a few days off his 56th birthday and his robust build had always given the impression of a man in the best of health.

The shock of Chapman's death showed itself in the games that followed. Arsenal lost three out of four and were knocked off the top of the First Division. But as after the setback at Walsall the previous season, they were soon back in form. In the spirit which was to carry post-Munich Manchester United to Wembley more than two decades later, Arsenal again won the League title.

Perhaps it was fitting that that season, the League was headed by Arsenal and Huddersfield, the two clubs whose destinies were so shaped by Chapman.

Chapman was succeeded at Arsenal by George Allison, who had been a director of the club and a well-known radio commentator on soccer. The club achieved League success in 1934 with 59 points and 75 goals, a considerable drop on the previous seasons. The momentum established by Chapman was still very much in evidence in the 1934–35 season. Allison had inherited a great team with some adjustments necessitated by retirement and the odd loss of form, he kept the honours rolling in to Highbury with League titles successes in 1935 and 1938.

Action around the Sheffield Wednesday goal during a 2–2 draw in 1935.

Following pages *The 1927 Cup Final squad, pictured at Highbury on April 22. Top Row, left to right: Cope, Baker, Parker, Lewis, Butler, John, Kennedy, Seddon. Bottom Row: Tom Whittaker (trainer), Hulme, Buchan, Brian, Blythe, Hoar, Herbert Chapman*

Alex James, playing his other favourite sport.

The Sheffield Wednesday goal under pressure during a League match at Highbury in 1936.

Ted Drake's goal clinches the 1936 Cup Final.

One of the first great names to go was David Jack, who became manager of Southend. Among the new arrivals was a fearless centre forward from Southampton called Ted Drake. He proved to be one of Allison's best buys as Arsenal once again hit the goal trail. In achieving only the second hat-trick in League history after Huddersfield, Arsenal scored 115 goals and conceded only 46. Their defence was even more unyielding that season, with the addition of two of the best wing halves ever to play for the club, Wilf Copping and Jack Crayston. As in the previous season, Arsenal went out of the Cup in the sixth round, 1935 was a historic year not just for the hat-trick. In an England international against Italy at Highbury, Arsenal provided a record contingent of seven players, Moss, Male, Hapgood, Copping, Bowden, Drake and Bastin.

The 1935–36 season saw Chapman's tradition continued, this time in the Cup, which they won for the second time by beating Sheffield United 1–0 with a goal by Drake. It had been quite a season for him. Although Arsenal finished only sixth in the League, in one match against Aston Villa they won 7–1 and Drake scored all seven – a First Division record which still stands.

In the seasons leading up to the Second World War, injuries and old age were to take their toll. Drake suffered from recurring cartilage trouble and the 1936–37 season was to be the last for James. In the circumstances Arsenal did well to finish third after a disastrous start, while in the Cup they went out in the quarter finals to West Bromwich Albion. James' retirement marked another watershed in the history of the club. With Chapman and Whittaker, who was rated as the greatest trainer of his day, James was one of the triumvirate who in the space of a decade had propelled Arsenal to the pinnacle of British football.

Alf Kirchen in action for Arsenal against Leeds in 1937.

'Wee' Alex is remembered as one of the game's all-time greats, a man with brilliant ball control and an uncanny sense of timing for the perfect pass. In addition to his first time balls out to Hulme, he was encouraged by Chapman to use the pass inside the full-back for the wingers to run on to. He also had a great sense of humour. He was very taken by a cartoon portraying him in baggy shorts and immediately went out and bought the biggest and baggiest pair he could find. He made them his own trademark.

Allison, meanwhile, continued to groom and sign some very good players. He lacked Chapman's man-management qualities and distanced himself from the players, happy to let Whittaker and his assistant, Joe Shaw, take charge of team affairs. But he had learned enough from the old master to satisfy the fans' expectation of success. In 1937–38, Arsenal again won the championship, for the fifth time in eight seasons. With only 52 points, one more than Wolves, with whom they'd fought a tight duel for the title, Arsenal's performance that season was not held in the same high regard as those which had gone before. But there were some encouraging features. Captain and full-back Hapgood was still in masterful form. While at centre half Arsenal had a new giant making his mark in the place of Herbie Roberts, for so long the bedrock of their defence. This was Bernard Joy, an amateur with Casuals and Arsenal, who 12 months earlier had won an England cap against Belgium. Like so many others, Joy's career was to be cut short by the outbreak of the Second World War.

Two more names making their presence felt were the Compton brothers, Denis and Leslie. While Denis, an outside left, went on to become one of England's foremost cricketers, full-back Leslie concentrated on football and was eventually to earn international honours with England.

One position Allison found hard to fill was that of James at inside left. The

Arsenal outside right Alf Kirchen beats Huddersfield goalkeeper Hesford in the 1–1 draw at Highbury in 1937.

man brought in to replace him was Bryn Jones, a record £14,500 buy from Wolves. Like James, Jones had been a goal-taker rather than a goal-maker, but unlike James was never given time to reproduce his best form at Highbury. In the last full season before the Second World War Arsenal finished on a quiet note. They were knocked out of the Cup in the third round by Chelsea and managed only fifth place in the League. The great decade of success started by Chapman came to a halt as the outbreak of war placed an untimely bookend against the greatest chapter in Arsenal's history.

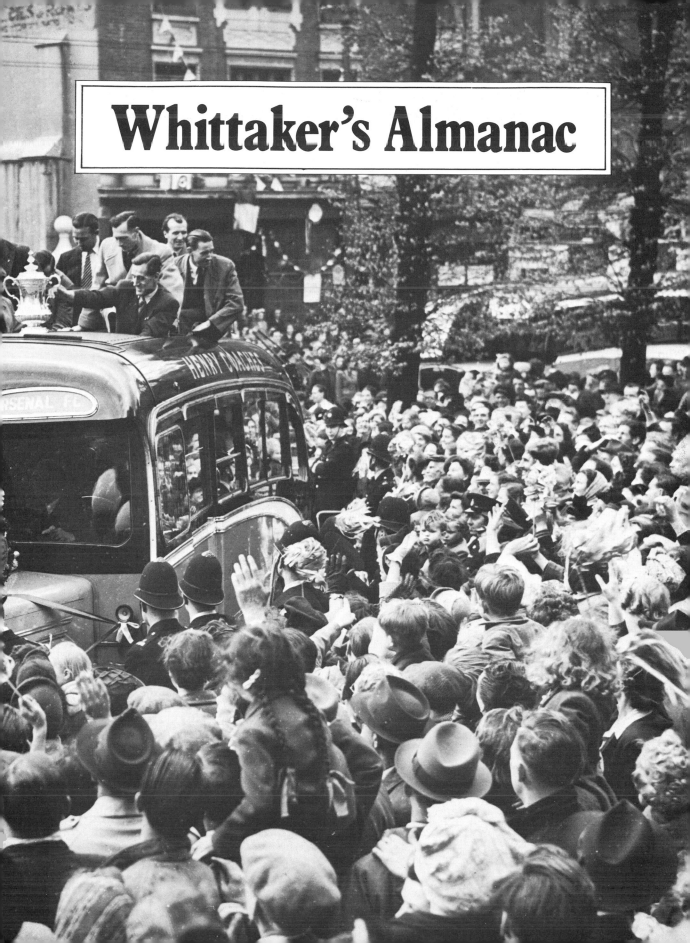

Whittaker's Almanac

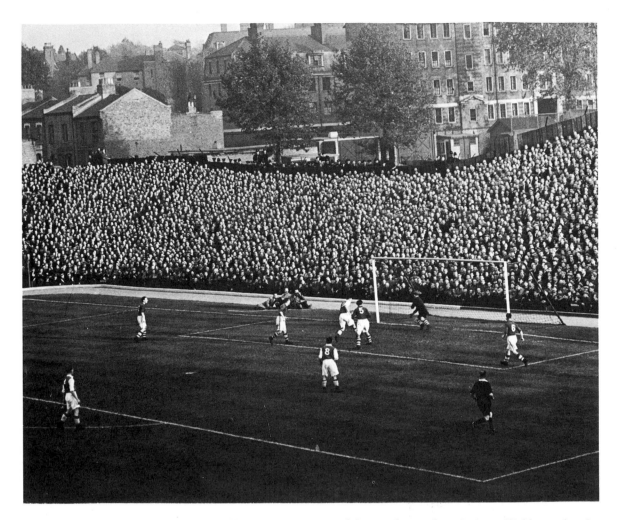

Post-war Action at Highbury as Reg Lewis scores for Arsenal in a 1–1 draw against Everton in 1947.

Preceding pages *Home the heroes... the fans salute the 1950 Cup winners.*

Rebuilding, in every sense of the word, was the priority at Highbury after the war. The famous stadium, which had been shut down and used as an Air Raid Precaution station, had been extensively damaged by incendiary bombs. On the field virtually a new squad of players were about to experience their own baptism of fire as League soccer got under way again. For Arsenal it was the age of uncertainty. The curtain had come down on the Chapman era with critics forecasting the club's demise. The disappointing results in 1938-39, the loss to war service of so many distinguished players and the almost impossibly high standards the club had set itself did not augur well for the future. Yet, remarkably, within two years the critics were proved wrong. Chapman's torch had been passed to a new generation of Gunners. At their head was Tom Whittaker, who had served his apprenticeship under first Chapman and then Allison and was now about to become a master builder in his own right. Whittaker was the last of the Chapman dynasty to scale the heights of League and Cup success. Between 1948 and 1953, Arsenal won two more championships, taking their total to a record seven, and reached two Wembley finals, winning one of them.

As with the outset of the Chapman era, there was little indication of the triumphs to come when League soccer recommenced in 1946. Arsenal had been obliged to play wartime games as the uneasy guests of neighbouring Spurs. When Highbury reopened for business, several players still hadn't returned from service, and those who were available, like Cliff Bastin and George Male had barely a season left in first class football. It was Bastin's 16th year at Arsenal and along with Male, who was captaining the club again for the first time in seven years, he was the last of the Chapman legends still in action at Highbury.

Despite George Allison resuming his duties as manager, with Whittaker back as his assistant after serving in the RAF as squadron leader, Arsenal made a disastrous start. They lost their opening game 6-1 to Wolves and for the early part of the season hovered just above the relegation zone. They were rescued mainly thanks to the arrival of two players, Ronnie Rooke and Joe Mercer. Rooke was 35 and thought to be over the hill when Allison bought him from Fulham to breathe new life into Arsenal's attack. Mercer was a tough-tackling wing half who was an England international with Everton. He had fallen from favour on Merseyside but Arsenal were quick to recognise what a great impact he could make at Highbury.

Inspired by Mercer, and with 21 goals in 24 games from Rooke and a season's total of 29 from their pre-War centre forward Reg Lewis, Arsenal turned the corner to finish the season relieved merely to be in 13th position. The title was won that year by Liverpool, helped by a youngster called Bob Paisley.

The 1947-48 season saw Whittaker's elevation to the post of manager as Allison retired. With his qualifications to manage the world's most famous soccer club given the added distinction of the MBE for his wartime service, Whittaker was excellently equipped for the role. Within a season he had reaped his first reward. Continuing the reconstruction of the side in the best Chapman tradition, he made some very shrewd acquisitions. The difference was that while Chapman spent money the club didn't have, Whittaker was able to profit from the post-War boom in crowds and gate revenue. Attendances of more than 50,000 packed Highbury for each home game and Whittaker gave them something to shout about. Brentford (and later Scotland) right half Archie Macaulay

Tom Whittaker holds court in the Arsenal dressing room.

was signed for £10,000, winger Don Roper came from Southampton and another outstanding wing half, Alex Forbes, arrived from Sheffield United. With Leslie Compton dominating the centre of defence, and Laurie Scott and Walley Barnes establishing themselves as the best full-back combination in the country, Whittaker, like Chapman before him, built success around a watertight defence. A mere 32 goals conceded was the best defence record in the club's history – only bettered by the Double year's 29 – as Arsenal powered to another League title. There were no slouches in attack, either, where Rooke scored 33 in 42 games, including one with his chin. Arsenal led the table from the start and despite the setback of going out of the Cup at home in the third round to Second Division Bradford, ran away with the championship with a month of the season still to play.

It was a magnificent achievement for Whittaker in his first season and although the following one was to prove a disappointment; it wasn't long before Arsenal were chalking up another triumph. The 1948-49 season saw the arrival from Walsall of the tall and powerful forward Doug Lishman but on the field Arsenal could manage no better than fifth behind the champions from Portsmouth. In the Cup, the fourth round brought defeat at the hands of Derby.

It's a goal...Arsenal on the way to victory in the 1950 Cup Final.

While Portsmouth then carried off the League title for the second season in succession, Arsenal made their mark in 1950 on the FA Cup.

It was the year when the cries of 'Lucky Arsenal' once again echoed round the country as the Gunners were drawn at home in every round – indeed they never left London during the entire competition. With the squad strengthened by the addition of goal-scorer Peter Goring from Cheltenham and the versatile Freddie Cox from neighbouring Spurs – one of the few bits of business transacted between the two North London rivals – Arsenal reached the semi-finals conceding only one goal. They beat Sheffield Wednesday 1-0, Swansea 2-1, Burnley 2-0 and Leeds 1-0. Their goalkeeper was the courageous and dependable George Swindin, Scott and Barnes at full-back (with Lionel Smith commanding some occasional appearances), a half-back line of Forbes and Mercer with Compton as a deep-lying centre-half, and a forward line of Cox, Goring, Lewis, Logie and, when he wasn't scoring Test centuries for England, Denis Compton on the left wing. Although he'd joined the club just before the war, Scotsman Logie was another of those young enough and lucky enough to have come through the barren years to mature into a great player. He was Arsenal's post-War Alex James, a little man with a massive football talent. Like James he was an inside left with

brilliant ball skills which were the inspiration behind the triumphs of 1948, 1950 and 1953.

Arsenal's opponents in the semi-final at White Hart Lane were Chelsea, who were strongly fancied to win. That feeling seemed to be vindictated when Chelsea took a 2-0 lead in the first half. But luck was certainly on Arsenal's side when Cox curled in a corner seconds before half-time. Perhaps he knew something about the air turbulence at his old ground, for the ball skimmed the heads of the Chelsea defence and appeared to be almost sucked into the goal at the near post. Arsenal came out for the second half a revitalised side and once again it was their irrepressible sense of adventure which helped to snatch a dramatic equaliser. Although he'd been waved back by skipper Joe Mercer, big Leslie Compton couldn't resist the temptation to power into the goalmouth for a corner taken by his brother Denis. The two timed their act to perfection as Leslie homed in to send a flying header into the back of the net.

In the replay it was Cox who provided an extra time encore, scoring the only goal of the game to send Arsenal back to Wembley for a fifth FA Cup Final. Their position of sixth in the First Division had its compensations after all.

Whittaker showed his flair in the preparations for the Final, in which Arsenal faced Liverpool. Because the two teams traditionally played in red strip, they were both obliged to change colours for Wembley. But because the change strip for each happened to be white, another change was necessary and it was Arse-

Captain Joe Mercer receives the Cup from King George VI.

The victorious 1950 Cup side.

nal who found themselves having to choose a new colour scheme. Whittaker came up with the most eye-catching combination he could think of: old gold, black and white for everyone except goalkeeper George Swindin, who was kitted out in a brilliant crimson jersey. Apart from crimson being the nearest permissible thing to Arsenal's original colour, Whittaker figured that such a conspicuous sight might distract the Liverpool forwards. The Arsenal manager's biggest problem was in choosing his centre forward. Lishman was the young pretender to the position with some excellent League performances, but Lewis was the regular Cup incumbent and with Peter Goring, who had scored 21 goals in his debut season, was leading marksman. Whittaker decided that Lewis's big match temperament would be better suited to Wembley and his judgment proved absolutely correct. Lewis scored twice and Joe Mercer was carried shoulder-high round Wembley parading the Cup. It was a great day for the Comptons, too, with Denis and Leslie sharing in Arsenal's triumph. In retrospect it was a poignant occasion, too, for Denis retired from football a few days later and Leslie played only a handful more games.

If good luck played a part in Arsenal's 1950 Cup run, it was bad luck which almost certainly deprived them of a seventh League title in 1951. Lishman had established himself in the forward line and had scored 16 goals by Christmas, including two hat-tricks, as Arsenal topped the table. Then tradgedy struck. In the Christmas Day game against Stoke he broke a leg and was out for virtually the remainder of the season. Arsenal's form suffered and they finished the season fifth while the League title went to White Hart Lane. There were some new arrivals at Highbury that season who were to make a major impact in defence and attack over the coming year. Goalkeeper Jack Kelsey was signed from the Welsh club Winch Wen, and wing half and fellow Welshman Dave Bowen joined from Northampton. Other newcomers were a tall, powerfully built player called Cliff Holton, from Oxford City, and a fair-haired winger who continued the soccer-cricket tradition at Highbury. This was the Gloucestershire and England batsman Arthur Milton.

Tom Whittaker and a trophy cabinet full of silverware on Highbury's first floor.

The 1951-52 season saw Arsenal again challenging for both major honours and for the second season in succession suffering telling injury blows. They scored 15 goals with only two against in reaching the semi-finals of the FA Cup and 40 goals from Lishman (23) and Holton (17) powered them to joint top of the First Division with Manchester United with only two matches remaining. In the Cup they were once again paired with their old sparring partners from Chelsea in the semi-final. And inevitably it was Freddie Cox, the scourge of the Blues at White Hart Lane two years previously, who inflicted further damage. Returning to the same stage where he had starred in 1950, Cox scored in the 1-1 draw which led to yet another replay and then scored twice in the 3-0 win which took Arsenal to Wembley for their sixth FA Cup Final. Meanwhile in the League, injuries to Leslie Compton and their outstanding new wing half Ray Daniel, and a bout of blood poisoning which laid low Lishman and Logie, dealt a devastating blow to Arsenal's championship attempt. With United winning and Arsenal losing their penultimate game, Whittaker's men needed a 7-0 win in the final game of the season at Old Trafford to turn the tables. Whittaker had already conceded the title when the two sides met and United's 6-1 victory was emphatic confirmation.

Whittaker was involved in a race against time to get his walking wounded fit for the Cup Final against Newcastle, who were going for their second consecutive Wembley victory. Daniel was only just out of plaster on a broken wrist, Logie was very doubtful and Roper was recovering from a thigh strain. All three played, but 19 minutes into the game disaster struck. Walley Barnes, their gallant Welsh full-back, received a crippling knee injury and had to come off. Ten-man Arsenal battled on with the score goalless until late in the second half. Then after Lishman clipped the bar in the nearest either side had come to scoring, George Robledo scored for Newcastle. It was all over. Arsenal had lost. Whittaker told his men he was prouder of them in defeat than he ever had been in victory.

George Robledo scores the only goal in the 1952 Cup Final watched by Newcastle team-mate Jackie Milburn (No 9).

Preceding pages *Pat Jennings – like good wine, he got better with age.*

No sooner had the dust settled on that season than Arsenal were once again in pursuit of major honours. Jack Kelsey forced his way into the goalkeeper's jersey, which he was to wear with distinction for a decade, Joe Wade enjoyed a run at left back in place of Barnes, and Milton played on the right wing.

The half-back line read: Forbes, Daniel, Mercer, while the forward line comprised Milton, Logie, Holton, Lishman and Goring or Roper. Although they were knocked out of the Cup in the quarter finals by Blackpool, who went on to win at Wembley in the famous Matthews Final, Arsenal took their challenge for the League title to the very last game of the season. Lishman and Holton had already scored more than 40 goals between them when the Gunners stepped out against Burnley on a monsoon-like First of May needing victory to shade Preston for the title on goal average. More than 50,000 fans packed Highbury for a nail-biting encounter in which Burnley made everyone's heart sink by taking an eighth minute lead. But within a further 12 minutes Arsenal had stormed back to go 3-1 ahead with goals by Forbes, Logie and Lishman. A late reply from

Tommy Lawton playing for the Gunners in 1954.

Burnley brought the fans to the edge of their seats but Arsenal held on to triumph 3-2. The title was back at Highbury for a record seventh time by a fraction of a goal. Both sides had 54 points, Arsenal had scored 97 for with 64 against while Preston's tally read 85-60. That's how close it was.

Whittaker had now emulated Chapman and Allison in terms of material success. Perhaps his sides lacked the explosive and spontaneous genius of the Chapman era but names like Mercer, Forbes, the Comptons, Logie, Lishman and Holton will live forever in the annals of Arsenal. The 1952-53 season was a milestone in the club's history, not only for the title win. Just as suddenly as Whittaker's success story began, so also did it end. Unlike the Chapman era, which was halted by the War, Whittaker's triumphs came to a stop through injury and old age. As Tottenham's Bill Nicholson was to remark more than a decade later as the Glory Glory team began to break up, soccer runs in cycles. The trick is to try to break the cycle by replacing players before they get old. Many of Whittaker's men had their best days behind them, and although the Arsenal manager had almost unlimited resources with which to buy replacements, clubs were refusing to part with their star Players for any price. Men like Stanley Matthews, John Charles and Jack Froggatt were on the wanted list at Highbury but either the clubs wouldn't sell or, in Froggatt's case, the player was reluctant to join. The 1953 title win was to prove Arsenal's last major honour for seventeen years.

The 1953-54 season began sadly with the death of Alex James. Then in a game against Liverpool, Joe Mercer broke his leg and was out of football for good.

Trying to repeat his success with Rooke, Whittaker signed 34-year-old Tommy Lawton, the great England centre forward from Brentford, in a bid to revitalise the attack, and Welshman Derek Tapscott arrived as a goal-scoring inside forward. Arsenal finished the season a disappointing 12th and went out of the Cup in the 4th round. Jimmy Logie had now retired and there was no one to fill the

Goalmouth action at Highbury as Arsenal take on Preston.

Tommy Docherty, who became Arsenal's midfield dynamo in the late 1950s.

Don Howe, Arsenal and England full-back during the early Sixties.

Preceding pages *Liam Brady, Irish midfield genius of the Seventies.*

position which had been at the heart of Arsenal's success over the previous 25 years. In 1956 Whittaker died, like Chapman, in service with the club which had been his life. He was Arsenal's third manager in 30 years. In the course of the next ten, they were to have four as the search for old glories took a heavy toll on those entrusted with the task. Jack Crayston and George Swindin, both former players, managed competently but not to the degree of excellence required. The highest position achieved in this period was 3rd in 1958–59, when the club found an inspirational wing half from Preston in Tommy Docherty. Other players, like Danny Clapton, David Herd, Jimmy Bloomfield, Vic Groves and Geoff Strong made their individual marks but the side as a whole rarely clicked. In 1960 the arrival of George Eastham from Newcastle at last gave Arsenal an inside forward with the skills and generalship of Logie. Even then the team's performance failed to push Arsenal higher than mid-table. In 1962 the club broke with tradi-

Cliff Holton scores against a Brazilian touring side in a friendly at Highbury in 1954.

tion by appointing a man with no previous managerial experience. Former Wolves and England captain Billy Wright had retired only three-years previously after winning a record 105 international caps. He came amid a fanfare of publicity – but his Highbury honeymoon was short-lived.

However in his four-year reign Wright did lay the foundation stones of the phenomenal Double triumph which was to come at the turn of the decade. His development of the youth team saw the recruitment of players like Ray Kennedy, Peter Simpson, Peter Storey, Jon Sammels and Pat Rice, who were all to play a major part in the success of the seventies. He bought the future Double captain, Frank McLintock, from Leicester in 1964, and buys like Joe Baker, Ian Ure, Terry Neill and Don Howe gave Arsenal a nucleus of quality if only moderate League positions. But when the club slipped to 14th in the 1965-66 season – their lowest League position in 36 years – the writing was on the wall for Wright.

Billy Wright, whose four-year reign ended in the sack.

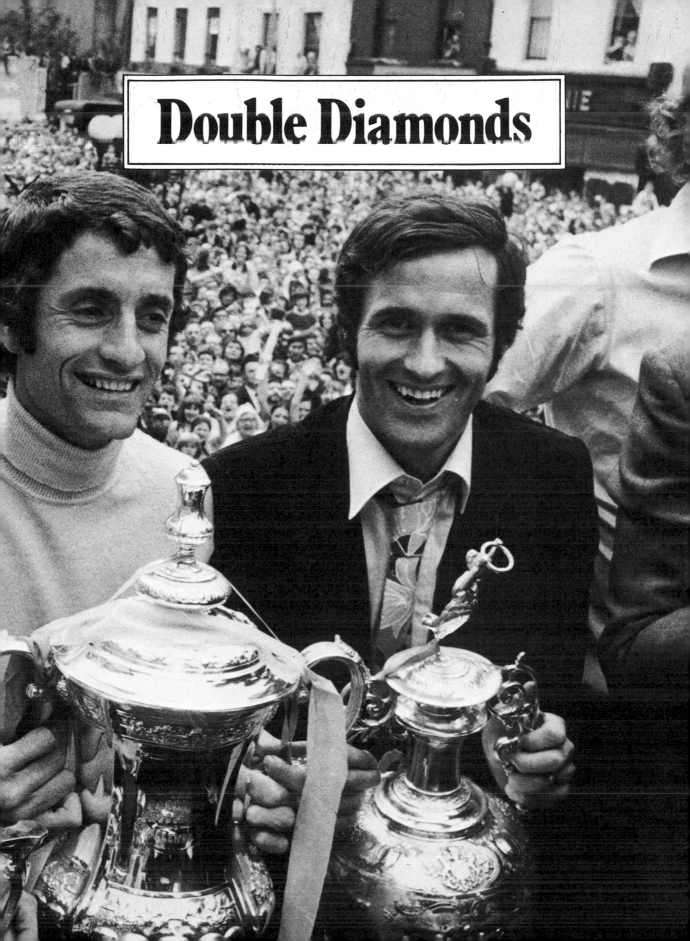

Double Diamonds

*Opposite Charlie
George...darling of the North
Bank during the Double era.*

Preceding pages *Charlie
George, Frank McLintock and
George Graham with the three
trophies Arsenal won in 1971: the
FA Youth Cup, the FA Cup and
the League championship trophy.*

Nobody will ever forget the afternoon Bertie Mee's Arsenal finally strode out from under the shadow of Herbert Chapman's immortals. The sun shone, in fact it blazed down on them at Wembley during two hours of dramatic but exhausting combat in May, 1971 when they came from behind to defeat Liverpool in extra time and clinch the treasured League and FA Cup double.

Like climbing Everest, many had tried but failed and only a very special team could hope to succeed. The task demanded an almost unique brand of determination, experience, skill and organisation. Arsenal, driven and inspired by one of the great captains in Frank McLintock, had all these qualities in abundance plus some vital ounces of luck to become only the second club in the 20th century to reach soccer's twin summit.

The first had been the celebrated Tottenham side of exactly a decade earlier and strangely Arsenal's place in the record books rested squarely on them beating their neighbours in the last League game four days before the Cup Final. This time the venue was the cauldron of White Hart Lane, brought to the boil by age old rivalry and the importance of the occasion. Make no mistake, Tottenham, who finished third in the League that season, were hell bent on stopping the old enemy.

On one of the most memorable nights for football in North London more than 51,000 fans packed into the ground and as many more were locked out in the nearby streets as Arsenal sought the goalless draw which would give them the title for a record eighth time and pip Don Revie's favourites from Leeds at the post. Ray Kennedy, a powerhouse of a centre forward even at 19, made sure they went one better when he headed the most important of his 26 goals that season in the final minute.

Against Liverpool with the score 1–1 and a replay looming, another youngster to come through the Highbury ranks proved the FA Cup winner with an unforgettable goal. Charlie George, blessed with marvellous yet enigmatic natural talent, looked on the threshold of greatness that day as did the Arsenal team. Yet the seeds for the club's greatest triumph had been sown five years earlier when Charlie, the fan from around the corner in Holloway, had found it hard to raise a cheer on the North Bank.

The four disappointing years under the management of Billy Wright climaxed in the acrimonious 1965-66 season when Arsenal were a club at war – with themselves and the fans. Midway through the season, as a very average team failed to make any impact, England internationals Joe Baker and George Eastham were granted transfers after being dropped. A month later in February, Nottingham Forest paid their record fee of £65,000 for Baker. There were no enquiries for Eastham.

In March, skipper Don howe broke his leg during a goalless draw with Blackpool at Highbury. Even that tragedy for the former England full-back could not quell the demonstrations by angry fans during the game and afterwards outside the club's offices.

Arsenal had never scrambled higher than seventh during Wright's reign. The old aristocrats had hit the hardest times of their unbroken 54-year stay in the First Division. At the home match with Leeds one supporter brought a bugle to play the Last Post but there were not many with him to administer the last rites, - 4,554, the lowest First Division crowd since the First World War.

Wright, the former golden boy of English football, found his playing pedigree no qualification for one of the toughest jobs in football. By the end this pleasant and agreeable man was almost buried by the abuse. Wright must go, said the banners and the board eventually gave in, ending his first and last venture into management just six weeks before England staged the World Cup Finals.

With the country in the thrall of that momentous competition, Arsenal's decision to promote Bertie Mee, their trainer of six years, to acting manager passed

*Bertie Mee who succeeded Billy
Wright.*

by almost unnoticed. Those that read the few paragraphs detailing his appointment could be forgiven for thinking that he was only keeping the seat warm for a more illustrious successor. Even the players were slightly incredulous that the martinet of the treatment room could revitalise Arsenal.

At 46, this dapper little man came to the job with no track record as a player, only part-time war service with Derby and Mansfield as a nippy outside left. Although injury put him out of the game soon after, he admits he would never have made a First Division player. He had no background of managerial success, having joined Arsenal as a physio' in 1960. But the leadership skills he honed as a captain in the RAMC were to be translated into his new environment. So too were the psychological insights into the professional footballer's mind he had gathered during all those years treating injuries. Here, indeed, was another Tom Whittaker.

For the next ten years, Mee was to fully justify this assessment by his chairman Denis Hill-Wood: 'Bertie's a hard, shrewd, little man, full of character and pride. He's nobody's fool and a man-manager of the highest class.'

He also recognised his own weaknesses and although possessing a full FA coaching badge nearly always worked in tandem with a first-class young coach. His initial move to strengthen the staff that summer was not on the playing side

George Armstrong tackles Chelsea's John Dempsey

but to bring in one of the brightest young coaches in the game from Fulham. Dave Sexton was his name and the players responded greedily to his ideas and philosophy.

Mee inherited a team which surprisingly featured six of the eventual Double side – McLintock, still an attacking wing half, winger George Armstrong, forwards John Radford and Jon Sammels plus defenders Peter Simpson and Peter Storey. Goalkeeper Bob Wilson, who had joined the club as an amateur, and young full-backs Pat Rice and Sammy Nelson were also on the staff. The initial task as Mee saw it was to instil discipline and pride. 'There's been a tendency in the last three or four years for the opposition to think that if they work at Arsenal and get a goal they will collapse. That must change and only teamwork earns anything worthwhile.', he said.

Sexton explained how: 'Every player regardless of position has obligations to attack and defend. There is a need for exceptional fitness, unselfishness, commitment and team spirit'. Five years on Sexton could easily have been talking of the double side.

Bob Wilson, the Double keeper.

Within a month of the new season starting two more vital components had arrived. George Graham, a tall and stylish striker later to excel in midfield, came from Chelsea in a deal that took reserve Tommy Baldwin and £50,000 to Stamford Bridge. Then two days later Mee stepped into transfer talks between Huddersfield and Liverpool to persuade Bob McNab to move south. The British club record of £50,000 for a full-back was well spent for the cheerful McNab was not only an astute tackler but read the game beautifully and was to become a vital supporting influence to McLintock when he took over the captaincy from Terry Neill in 1969.

By February, the Arsenal revival was well and truly under way. 'There's something in the air at Highbury', said Mee, and the board agreed with him by confirming him as manager and promoting Sexton to be his assistant. The settled atmosphere was underlined by George Armstrong's decision to stay with the club he had joined from school. The little winger had been unsettled for two years but like many he saw a new era dawning and he was to make over 500 appearances for the club, the most by this generation of players. He reached the peak of his career during the Double year. A player of boundless energy, he scored goals, made goals and helped stop goals and his ability to be two players in one was a priceless asset.

Mee's first season ended with a run to the fifth round of the FA Cup and seventh in the First Division behind champions Manchester United, a glittering side inspired by the genius of George Best.

During the next two seasons, 1967–68 and 1968–69, the team came within touching distance of their first major trophy since the 1953 championship only to suffer the heartbreaking disappointment of being Wembley losers in rapid succession. But just as the first League Cup run was getting under way and the fans were celebrating a shifting of the balance of power in North London following a 4-0 defeat of Spurs, the camp was rocked by the departure of the much-respected Sexton, who was tempted back to manage his first love Chelsea when they dispensed with the services of Tommy Docherty.

Sexton was a hard act to follow and Arsenal's decision to promote Don Howe at 31 from player to coach was met with hostility by the team. Howe's career had been finished by his broken leg but the players soon discovered that here was another brilliant coach in the making, a good motivator bursting with original ideas. He soon earned their respect and Highbury began to buzz as the cup run gathered momentum. First Division newcomers Coventry were overcome 2-1 in a tricky away tie and then wins over Reading, Blackpool and Burnley brought them to a two leg semi-final against Bob McNab's old club. Huddersfield were struggling in the Second Division and a final date with mighty Leeds was sec-

George Graham...the strolling player in Arsenal's midfield during the early Seventies.

Pat Rice, one of Arsenal's best defenders.

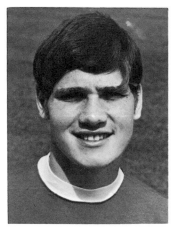

ured by 3-1 wins home and away.

The League Cup was still in its infancy and the First Division rivals gave the second Wembley final respectability. Arsenal's presence also guaranteed a full house.

In the event, two well-organised sides cancelled each other out and provided one of Wembley's stinkers which was decided by a controversial goal from Leeds full back Terry Cooper, Arsenal claiming a foul on their goalkeeper. The big consolation for Leeds, so often the bridesmaids when it came to winning trophies, was that they ended a 63-year wait to win a piece of silverware. The small consolation for Arsenal was that they were the closest of any southern team to one of the big prizes. The FA Cup went to West Bromwich and the championship, in which Arsenal finished ninth, was a battle for supremacy between the two Manchester clubs, Leeds and Liverpool and eventually won by City thanks to the attacking verve of Bell, Lee and Summerbee.

If losing to Leeds was a disappointment, being beaten as red-hot favourites the following year by Third Division Swindon was not far short of disaster, especially as Arsenal were growing in stature and good enough to finish fourth behind Leeds, champions this time. It was the Gunners' best League season since a rare top three finish in 1958–59.

The route to Wembley had been so enjoyable too. It included a 6–1 win at Scunthorpe, a 2–1 defeat of Liverpool and eventually a semi-final epic with Tottenham. John Radford's only goal of the game at Highbury in the first leg proved decisive because the Gunners held Spurs to a 1–1 draw at White Hart Lane, Radford cancelling out a Jimmy Greaves goal. The two games were watched by a

John Radford, tall target man.

total of 111,160 fans, more than Wembley could hold for the final when Arsenal, with six first teamers weakened by flu, must have wished an unusually heavy Wembley pitch would open up and swallow them as Swindon produced one of the great cup shocks.

Swindon, boasting the best side in their history, had beaten some good sides on the way and had even come through a semi-final play off with Burnley, who were still a power in the First Division. Swindon surprised everyone by rising to the occasion again with a two-goal performance from their home-grown winger Don Rogers plus some blinding saves from Peter Downsborough stirring memories of the famous Walsall cup debacle for Arsenal.

The Arsenal goalscorer that day was one Bobby Gould who was proving one of their expensive mistakes. One department still causing concern was goalscoring and Gould, a bustling centre forward who had scored 28 in Coventry's promotion to the First Division was signed a year earlier as a foil for George Graham. The fee – a record £90,000. The fans took a shine to the wholehearted Gould but at the highest level he lacked the necessary height and control. Gould was to disappear into the reserves at the start of the 1969–70 season and eventually moved

Eddie Kelly blasts one past Stoke's Gordon Banks back in the Double days.

on to Wolves nine months later after scoring only 16 goals in 57 appearances.

One of them, against Irish part-timers Glentoran, gave him an honourable mention in the Fairs Cup campaign, for despite their disappointment at Wembley, Arsenal made it into Europe for the first time on the strength of their League position. They joined holders Newcastle, Liverpool and Southampton in a competition in which they were to extend English domination in spectacular fashion.

But while they tasted triumph on foreign fields, they were treading a very shaky path at home and the success in Europe was in direct contrast to a disappointing domestic season in which the Gunners went out of the League Cup to Everton, were KO'd in an FA Cup third round replay by Second Division Blackpool after leading 2–0, and finished halfway down the table because they failed to turn superiority into goals, especially in 18 drawn games.

When Europe came around they were transformed. After brushing past Glentoran, Sporting Lisbon and Rouen were made to bite the dust and in the quarterfinals they dealt ruthlessly with the unknown quantity of Dinamo Bacau. Goals from Sammels and Radford in Rumania left the return a formality and with the

pressure off, Arsenal slammed home seven goals at Highbury, including the first two in European competition for the exciting George. Goalkeeper Bob Wilson, brave as a lion, had also established himself as No 1 five years after joining the club as a 23-year-old amateur, while an all action midfield player called Eddie Kelly had burst onto the scene at 19 years of age. The final pieces in the jigsaw were slotting into place.

One that didn't fit was Peter Marinello who arrived in January 1970 as London's answer to George Best. His hair was as long as the mercurial Irishman's and he possessed a hint of the magical ball skills but there the similarities ended. Arsenal paid out £100,000, for the first time, for a 19-year-old Scot who had only been in the game 18 months and who had none of the experience and physical resilience needed to survive in the tough world of the English First Division. He was prone to injury and dazzled by the bright lights and manager Mee was soon forced to drop him into the reserves to learn his trade because he was too much of a luxury. Marinello eventually came back to play half a season in the first team but he had become neither a natural, nor a team, player and he was eventually transferred to Portsmouth in 1975.

Don Howe had more success in converting the admirable McLintock from wing half to central defender, a move which initially was seen as the way to prolong the 29-year-old Scot's career and led to Arsenal having almost a perfect combination at the back for 18 months. Centre half Ian Ure, the big, blond-haired Scot had moved to Manchester United and club skipper Terry Neill was nearing the end of his career in the First Division. McLintock succeeded him and reluctantly agreed to the positional switch. But with the tactical guidance of Bob McNab on the field, he struck up a marvellous partnership with the tough tackling Peter Simpson which was to become not only the cornerstone of the Fairs Cup win but the double year to follow.

In the semi-finals, Arsenal showed their mettle by outplaying Ajax, Johan Cruyff and all, to the tune of 3–0 at Highbury and restricted the Dutchmen to 1–0 in Amsterdam. The measure of these performances is underlined by Ajax going on to win the European Cup at Wembley the following year.

But if Ajax were tough, Arsenal's opponents in the two-leg final were even more formidable. Anderlecht had accounted for Dunfermline and Newcastle and in their semi-final had beaten Inter Milan 3–0 on aggregate including a 1–0 win in Italy. They carried that form into the first leg of the final in Brussels and two goals from their Dutch centre forward Jan Mulders plus a third from Johan Devrindt looked like the end for Arsenal. But in a desperate bid for a vital goal to take to Highbury, Bertie Mee threw on young Ray Kennedy for Charlie George and as so often in his Arsenal career he came up with the goods, a header in the last few minutes to salvage hope for the return.

On the afternoon of the second leg UEFA gave Arsenal another boost by deciding that away goals would count double and despite a dismal, rainy night 51,612 packed into Highbury and cheered their heads off. Arsenal had felt, even in defeat, that when they had the bulk of the attacking the Belgians would not be able to cope with the pressure on their defence.

They bombarded Anderlecht for 20 minutes and then Kelly made the breakthrough with a shot from the edge of the area. One of a stream of crosses that night brought Arsenal level midway through the second half when McNab centred and Radford, scourge of the Belgians in the air, nodded in. Jon Sammels made sure that the cup was not won on a technicality by running in to convert a George pass and Highbury almost took off with excitement.

McLintock collected the cup, Bob Wilson did his own lap of honour and the team were submerged by delirious fans on the pitch. With hindsight both manager Mee and skipper McLintock admit that this night gave them even more pleasure than the double win because many of the fans that night had grown to manhood without seeing Arsenal win something. Now that had been put right in such exciting fashion.

The 1971 Double winning squad

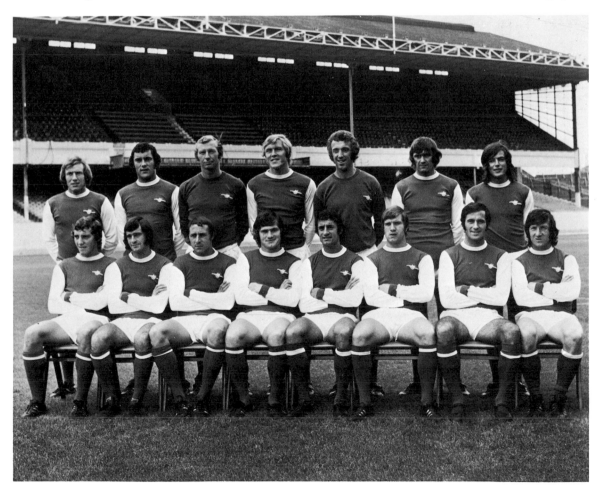

Charlie George...instant glory with the 1971 FA Cup-winning goal.

But had anyone predicted at the start of the 1970–71 season that this team was capable of winning the double as an encore, he would have been laughed out of Highbury. After the first game, a 2–2 draw with champions Everton at Goodison, they felt everything was against them. Simpson had collected a cartilage injury in pre-season training and an operation kept him out until November, Sammels cracked a bone in a warm-up match and George came back from Everton with a cracked bone in an ankle.

The injuries were a blessing in disguise, George's absence meant they had to introduce Kennedy as a regular partner for Radford up front while John Roberts replaced Simpson alongside McLintock at the back. The chemistry was right because the Radford-Kennedy combination brought goals and Roberts, a Wales centre half, was a superb stand-in. When George was fit again he was brought back into midfield and with the perfect pair up front, Mee and Howe were able to perm any three from five in midfield. The competition for places, so intense as the season progressed, was another important factor.

Before the season opened there was good news for their European ambitions when UEFA decided that, as holders, Arsenal could defend the Fairs Cup, even

though they had not finished high enough in the First Division to qualify. The bad news was drawing Lazio.

John Radford had hit a hat-trick against Manchester United and Leeds had dropped their first point in 12 with a goalless draw at Highbury before Arsenal set off for the first leg in Rome. It was a pretty hostile atmosphere and the team were feeling quite pleased with themselves after two more Radford goals cancelled out two from Giorgio Chinaglia. But as the players left the after-match dinner they were attacked in the street by their Lazio opponents who had been lying in wait. It turned into a brawl and Arsenal officials led by Mee somehow broke it up and bundled the players back onto the team bus. In one of the great understatements of all time the Lazio president put it down to, 'an excess of conviviality', but it was seen as one of the most disgraceful incidents so far in European football.

There were fears of more trouble in the return but the Lazio players decided to play football and Arsenal coasted through 2–0.

The following Saturday there was another shock to the system when Arsenal crashed 5–0 at Stoke; but this was not the fragile Gunners of old and they

George Graham celebrates as Eddie Kelly's equaliser goes in against Liverpool in the 1971 FA Cup Final.

bounced back with a 4–0 League Cup replay win over Ipswich before embarking on a league run that brought 25 out of 28 points by mid-January when they went down 2–1 at Huddersfield. The second leg of the double had also got under way with a 3–0 win on non-league Yeovil's slope, but in Europe all was not well. Sturm Graz beat them 1–0 in Austria and it needed Peter Storey's last minute penalty to give them a 2–1 aggregate win. Storey's penalty taking in moments of high tension was to prove invaluable again when he scored from the spot at Portsmouth in an FA Cup fourth round tie and then finished them off with another last minute penalty to make it 3–2 at Highbury.

Throughout the season all the smart money was on Leeds to win the title but the first signs of their vulnerability as leaders appeared in early February when John Toshack's winner for Liverpool inflicted a second successive home defeat on Don Revie's men. That day, Arsenal closed the gap to three points when John Radford's goal was good enough to beat Manchester City. And in the fourth round of the FA Cup Leeds suffered a major psychological blow when little Colchester beat them. No such problems for Arsenal, with Charlie George skating over the Maine Road snow for the two goals that knocked out Manchester City. It was away for the fifth round too at Leicester, the Second Division champions. They were held to a goalless draw and in the replay a 57,443 crowd saluted George as the matchwinner again.

A win double...Charlie George and Frank McLintock after the 1971 FA Cup win.

By this time, Arsenal's hold on the Fairs Cup had been loosened. They had seen off Beveren 4–0 but Cologne in the quarter-finals, helped by a farcical performance from Rumanian referee Petres, wrenched the trophy away. Arsenal won 2–1 at Highbury but the away goal was to prove fatal when the Germans clung on to a controversial penalty at home where the referee also decided he wanted the match played in silence as far as the players were concerned. The Arsenal players would never have believed that Mr Petres was actually doing them a favour, for out of Europe, they were able to concentrate solely on League and FA Cup. Championship rivals Leeds were still in the competition and even though they won it on penalties against Juventus to make up for losing the title, it must have proved a burden and distraction in the run-in.

Home the heroes after the Double

The Cologne disappointment was soon brushed aside as Arsenal turned their

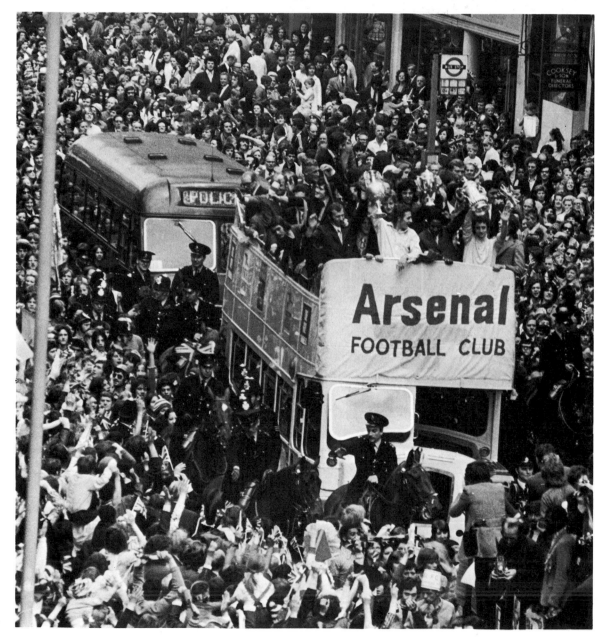

attention to an FA Cup semi-final with Stoke. On the day Liverpool made a second half comeback to beat old rivals Everton at Old Trafford while the Gunners breathed a huge sigh of relief when Peter Storey grabbed a replay with another last minute penalty: a Stoke defender handling a McLintock header on the line in Arsenal's last desperate attack. Unlike Stoke, Arsenal were not a side to let anyone back into a game and first half goals from Kennedy and Graham before a 62,500 crowd at the Villa Park replay earned the Wembley date.

Meanwhile the title race was hotting up, despite Leeds being eight points clear with eight to play. As April arrived two Kennedy goals gave Arsenal victory over Chelsea before Highbury's biggest crowd of the season – 62,987 – and George's winner at Newcastle sent the team to the top on goal average on the day Leeds lost 2–1 at home to West Brom, who hadn't won away from home for 16 months. Tony Brown's first goal, hotly disputed as offside, prompted a pitch invasion which brought a heavy fine for the time, £750, and an order to play the first four home games of the following season behind closed doors. Everyone saw the title decider as Leeds v Arsenal on April 26, but even though Jack Charlton's apparently offside goal gave the northerners victory, the Gunners were not to be denied. They needed only to avoid defeat at Tottenham a week later. Ray Kennedy made sure of that.

There was very little time to worry about Wembley and Liverpool. Arsenal's critics took great pleasure in condemning the team for lack of imagination – tight at the back and deliverers of highballs forward to Radford and Kennedy. But although Liverpool had conceded only 24 League goals they had broken no goalscoring records either with 42. Arsenal, with 71, were the second highest scorers and only one behind Leeds. The final turned into a war of attrition with the skills of George and Graham plus the silky running of Steve Heighway relieving the dour battle. Arsenal exerted most of the pressure but Liverpool held out and three minutes into extra time Heighway raced up the left wing and his shot beat the embarrassed Bob Wilson on his near post.

The equaliser came out of the blue. Tommy Smith and Emlyn Hughes dithered in their penalty area and Eddie Kelly swept the ball past Ray Clemence. Graham followed the ball in but TV proved it was Kelly's goal. And then a stunning climax. George, his legs weary and socks rolled down, moved forward, Radford laid the ball into his path 20 yards out and his rising right foot shot whistled past a despairing Clemence. Not many teams came from behind to beat Liverpool; even fewer did that to Arsenal. It was all over. George had written the last line in a major page of soccer history.

When skipper Frank McLintock lifted the Cup it was the first time he had been a Wembley winner in five cup finals. Arsenal skipper, new Footballer of the Year, soon to become an MBE, McLintock was the perfect example of the type of player who brought Highbury such momentous days. As Mee said, his players had great morale, great spirit and were great competitors. They had an inner drive.

Yet, it is still fashionable today to compare this Arsenal side unfavourably with Tottenham's double winners. But it is impossible to compare them. Arsenal came from eight points behind to win the League, were drawn away in each round of the Cup and plumbed the depths of their energy to come back and defeat Liverpool. Physically and mentally – even statistically – that is a far greater achievement. But comparisons are odious. Spurs were masters of the flowing football then in fashion, Arsenal were equipped to conquer the highly-trained modern teams to whom work rate was the first commandment.

On that day at Wembley, and even more so in a better performance as they won the league at Tottenham, Arsenal looked capable of dominating English football for a decade. Amazingly, within three months that dream was turning sour.

A New Generation

The euphoria of the Double win had hardly subsided when outside influences dealt Arsenal a heavy blow. Don Howe, their brilliant coach, had already rejected overtures from Leicester but a summer offer to take over West Bromwich, whom he had joined from school and for whom he had played more than 300 League games proved irresistible. Quite simply it gave him the chance to prove himself as a manager and not just a coach. Arsenal's chairman could understand his motive but West Bromwich's raid on the Highbury back room staff, which included FA Youth Cup-winning coach Brian Whitehouse, soured relationships. Happily for Arsenal and Howe the rift healed with time. To fill the coaching void, Arsenal promoted the reserve coach of four years, Steve Burtenshaw. He had sound ideas and belief in attacking football but he lacked the tough and inspirational sides of Howe's character and he walked into a situation with the players just as difficult as Howe had found after Sexton's departure five years earlier.

But for the players there was much to look forward to. McLintock felt they were capable of repeating the Double and there was the small matter of a tilt at the European Cup. Manchester United were still the only English club to have their name on the trophy.

As with the Double year, the season was preceded by a major injury blow. George, the Wembley hero was ruled out with cartilage trouble for two months. But there were no hints of a sudden decline when Chelsea, the new European Cup-winners Cup-holders, were swept aside 3-0 in the opening game. Yet by the end of August, the team had suffered three successive defeats including the first at home for 19 months when newly promoted Sheffield United numbered the Gunners among their surprise victims in a ten match unbeaten spell. Luckily, there was no serious opposition in the European Cup from Stromgodset of Norway who were beaten 7-1 over two legs and in the second round the 3-0 defeat of Grasshoppers stamped their passport to the quarterfinals. But the champions' form in the First Division was approaching crisis point and after crashing 5-1 at Wolves they found themselves ninth in the table by mid November. Like Leeds, Manchester City and Everton before them, they were finding it harder to retain the title than win it. Mee put his finger on the major problem by suggesting it was easy for one man to motivate himself again, but to motivate eleven others again...

Mee's remedies were drastic. Out went Simpson, McNab, Nelson and the recently restored George. Then, just before Christmas he paid a British record fee of £220,000 for Everton's inspirational midfield player Alan Ball. At 19, this flame-haired little terrier had helped win the World Cup and he matured to become a vital influence in Everton's title win of 1970. Ball, a master of the short passing give-and-take game, took time to settle into a team which relied so much on long balls but his galvanising effect was immediate. He launched the FA Cup run to Wembley with his first goal for the club in a 2-0 win at Swindon which gave many of his teammates sweet revenge for the League Cup Final defeat. The team, with George back in scoring form, went unbeaten in the First Division for 12 games until mid-February. Not only another double but a unique treble was in their sights. Yet Mee feared Ball had arrived a little too late and his ineligibility for the European Cup quarter final possibly cost the club another page in history.

To face the great Johan Cruyff, then at the peak of his powers, and holders Ajax, one of the great club sides of Europe, Arsenal had to rely on the brittle talents of Peter Marinello rather than the inspiration of Ball. But despite losing 2-1 in Amsterdam there was hope after a disciplined defensive performance. The Dutch masters were clearly worried and the injured Cruyff agreed to have five painkilling injections to play at Highbury. Arsenal's mistake was to try and batter talented opposition into submission. Ajax showed they could be resilient

Preceding pages Pat Jennings is beaten as Sammy McIlroy scores Manchester United's equaliser in the 1979 FA Cup Final.

Snowbound Highbury in 1970

too, successfully protecting a gift goal when Graham headed into his own net in a mix up with Wilson. Arsenal could draw some compensation from the fact that not only did Ajax retain the cup by beating Inter Milan but completed a hat-trick the following season in a golden era for Dutch football. The elimination came in the middle of three successive League defeats which effectively ended the title challenge too. The field was left to old rivals Leeds, Manchester City and Brian Clough's surprise packet from Derby. The FA Cup was Arsenal's last hope but after making it to the Centenary Final there was no happy ending against those old killjoys from Leeds. As so often in the past, the teams cancelled each other out in a physical battle littered with too many fouls. Despite Ball's best performance so far in Arsenal colours, Allan Clarke's header made it a third Wembley defeat for Arsenal in four years and a fifth and final losing visit for McLintock.

Leeds needed only to beat Wolves on the following Monday to win the Double themselves. But despite delaying their Cup-winning celebrations, the task proved too much for them and Arsenal had a final say in the title's destiny when they held Liverpool to a goalless draw at Highbury. Clough and his Derby players, en route to a holiday in Majorca, heard the news of the club's first major honour while flying 20,000 feet above the Mediterranean. After a season most clubs would envy Arsenal were in mourning and there was unrest in the camp. A wages row simmered among the younger players throughout the summer and the new season started with George and Kelly on the transfer list. There was more discontent when Mee paid £200,000 to Coventry in October for Jeff Blockley, a centre half in the big English stopper mould but a controversial replacement for the much respected McLintock, who felt his days at the top were far from over. November threw up another crisis. A 5-0 thrashing at Derby hard on the heels of a 3-0 League Cup defeat at home by Norwich brought matters to a head. Mee, privately stung by continual carping from an army of critics that Arsenal for all their success were not entertaining, had tried to turn them into the total footballers of Holland. But the experiment failed and it was decided to

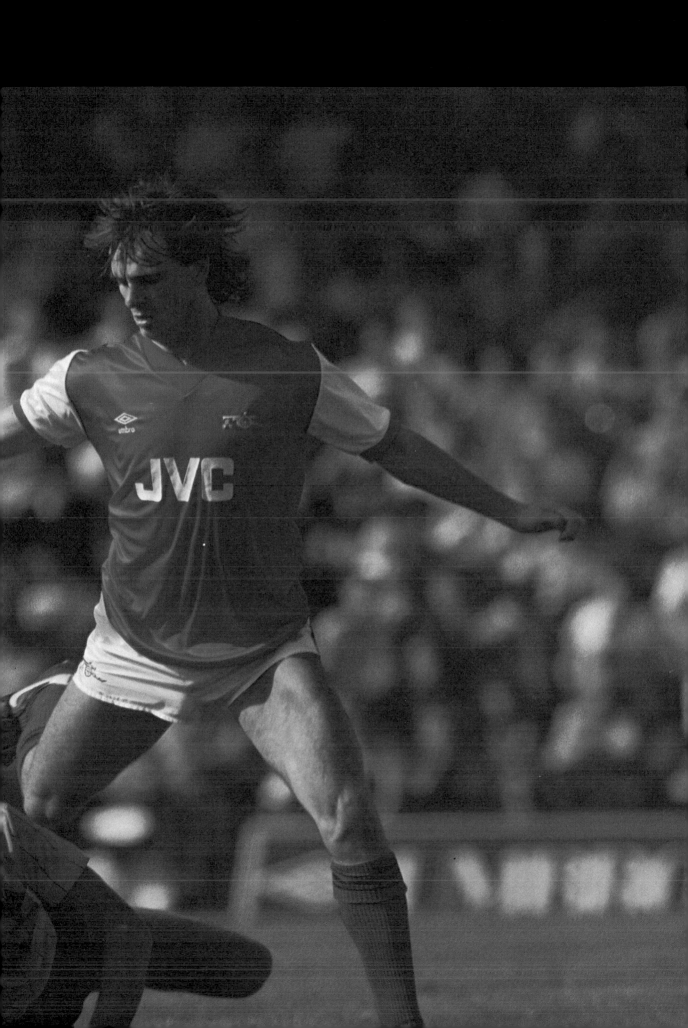

sacrifice popularity again in the cause of efficiency. The team responded by going 15 matches without defeat and with Radford and Kennedy back in harness they were chasing Liverpool for the title and heading for Wembley again. But this was a year in which romance defied logic for the umpteenth time in the cup. The semi-finals paired them with second division Sunderland and not only did Bob Stokoe's men dispose of the Gunners but shocked red hot favourites Leeds at Wembley in one of the most memorable finals. Mee, clearly bent on rebuilding, let two key men depart. McLintock, at 34, moved across London to QPR and had four more good years, taking them to within a whisker of the championship. Graham became Tommy Docherty's first target as manager of Manchester United and it was indicative of the unsettled mood at Highbury that the Scotland international felt in need of a fresh challenge.

There was another departure with the 1973-74 season only weeks old. Burtenshaw's brief reign as coach ended in resignation after two home defeats and a 5-0 beating at Sheffield United. The players had not been responding to him for a long time and it was an open secret that Mee wanted the extrovert 36-year-old Bobby Campbell who had helped Gordon Jago bring QPR up from the second division. But this was to be a season in which Arsenal fans had to fall back on their memories. The team were knocked out of the League Cup at home by little Tranmere and only in the last week of the season did they make a significant mark on the title race when Ray Kennedy's goal gave them victory at Anfield and confirmed Leeds as champions. Their old sparring partners had laid the foundations with an incredible 29-match unbeaten run. For Arsenal, down in tenth place, life could have been worse. Graham went down with Manchester United to the second division and Sir Alf Ramsey got the sack as England manager. Importantly for the future, a young Irishman called Liam Brady had forced his way into a struggling team, but there was a real sting in the tail. Goalkeeper Bob Wilson made his farewell appearance in the 1-1 draw with QPR but the night was marred by Ball breaking his leg.

There was a drastic rethink on tactics during the summer. The long ball game with Kennedy as a target man had not been working. The need was for fresh faces, fresh ideas and a fresh crusade. But Kennedy still had his admirers and the great Liverpool manager Bill Shankly made him his last signing before retiring, for £200,000. Arsenal spent half the Kennedy fee on Manchester United's abrasive Brian Kidd, another prodigy who had played in the European Cup-winning side. But although he became leading scorer with 19 goals in his first season he never forged a successful partnership with Radford.

Hopes that Ball could knit new and old personnel together crashed when he fractured his leg in a pre-season friendly and by the time he returned the new campaign had faltered badly. The unpopular Blockley and injury-prone George were on the transfer list – the defender moved to Leicester the following January – and an unsettled team sank to the bottom of the League accompanied by Tottenham during a run of ten games without a win. Mee surprised everyone with a move into the transfer market for QPR's 31-year-old defender Terry Mancini and it proved the best £20,000 outlay the manager ever made. The balding extrovert was good enough to make the Republic of Ireland team but Mee was looking as much for a psychological effect on the dressing room as stability in the heart of his defence. He got both and the team soon pulled out of their bad run but Mee was not so lucky with his next signing, Alex Cropley, a neat Scottish winger from Hibs who commanded a £150,000 fee. Cropley played only seven games before breaking his leg and he was never the same player again.

The FA Cup was proving a pleasant diversion to the struggles in the League and George Armstrong's first goals for 21 months saw them through a fifth round replay with Coventry. But controversy was never far away and in the

Ipswich's Brian Talbot and Malcolm Macdonald (right) battle in the 1978 FA Cup Final. Talbot later joined the Gunners.

Preceding pages *Frank Stapleton, scourge of defences, in the 1979 Cup Final*

League game at Derby, Ball and McNab were sent off. It was only the second occasion since the war that two players from the same side had been dismissed in the same match. The other time had involved Storey and McLintock in 1967. The club's decision not to support the players at an appeal – both were banned for three games – caused a rift between the club and Ball which was never really healed. Wembley seemed to be beckoning again but in the quarter final two goals from Alan Taylor, West Ham's FA Cup winning hero that season, produced another black day for Arsenal. It was the first time they had ever been beaten at home in the FA Cup by another London side. When the dust had settled, the fans faced the unthinkable fate of relegation. But the team fought like tigers to avoid the drop and finished 16th but they were too fierce for some. Ken Furphy, manager of Sheffield United said sadly after a 1-0 defeat at Highbury: 'I never thought I would see the day when Arsenal players fought among themselves, pulled shirts, wasted time and so freely indulged in foul tactics'. Desperate measures for desperate times...and elsewhere an old friend had lost the big battle. Don Howe's decline had been just as dramatic. West Brom had gone down the previous season, failed to bounce back and Howe's contract was not renewed.

The 1975-76 season marked the end of the Mee era but it proved a sad finale to one of the greatest periods in the club's history. The team, very much in transition, finished 17th behind Liverpool, their lowest position since 1925, and failed

Brian Talbot shoots Arsenal ahead against Manchester United in the 1979 FA Cup Final.

at the first hurdle in both cups. In the summer two more of the Double side departed, the controversial George almost joined Spurs but went to Derby for £90,000 and the admirable McNab went on a free transfer to Wolves. Ball went on the transfer list, Kelly was still unsettled but there were some consolations. Rice and Nelson were blossoming into a fine pair of full backs, David O'Leary had the look of a potential world class player on his debut, Frank Stapleton emerged as a promising and brave centre forward and Brady was casting an ever increasing influence on the team. But all the promise was not enough to prevent Mee bowing to the pressures after 10 unforgettable years. He was strongly influenced by his old friend Bill Nicholson, the man behind Tottenham's double winners. He had retired two years previously because he found he was not enjoying the job. Mee woke up one morning with the same feeling and that was the beginning of the end for him. When he announced his decision to the press he broke down in tears. It was the first time any of them had seen such a show of emotion – except a rare flash of anger – from this polite and reserved man. There was talk of him staying on as an adviser, even joining the board, but at the end of the season he left the club and was eventually to join Watford and help Graham Taylor take them into the first division.

But he will always be remembered as Arsenal's Double manager, the man who led them to five cup finals. Those were just the fruits of his works. He restored the pride, passion and power of a jaded giant of English football.

Initially Arsenal believed that there was nobody in English football to replace Mee but after an unsuccessful attempt to prise Yugoslav coach Miljan Miljanic away from Real Madrid, the speculation became intense. Brian Clough, Jack Charlton, Wales manager Mike Smith, Bolton's Ian Greaves were all names bandied about. The players wanted Campbell but in a dramatic month of July Terry Neill, the Gunners' former centre half, resigned from the Tottenham job in which he had succeeded Nicholson and took over the reins at Highbury. Neill had cut his teeth into management at Hull and also looked after the Northern Ireland side. At 35, this witty, articulate but steely operator behind the smile became Arsenal's youngest manager. Highbury needed a shake up and Neill was the man to make the sparks fly.

Campbell's position had been untenable and somewhat embarrassing for weeks and he left quietly. Neill brought his No 2 from Spurs Wilf Dixon but the dressing room was nervous and hostile and the new manager knew he had a tough job on his hands. But he was not a man to let the grass grow under his feet and the first of the spectacular moves into the transfer market which were his trademark came within days. Kidd had gone to Manchester City and to replace him at centre forward, Neill paid £333,333 for the swashbuckling Malcolm Macdonald from Newcastle. Gates had dropped from an average 40,000 in the Double year to 27,000 and Macdonald was seen as the initial step in providing a new exciting team to revive interest from the fans. He certainly did that, scoring 29 goals in his first season, including a hat-trick against his old club, and proving a vital influence on young Stapleton beside him in attack. Behind them the midfield of Brady, Trevor Ross and Ball was inventive but defensively Arsenal were still very brittle. Things were improving but hardly a week went by without the club hitting the headlines. In December Ball moved to Second Division Southampton and Neill took a massive risk on bringing Alan Hudson back to London from Stoke for £200,000. Hudson, who had made his name with Chelsea as one of the most skilful midlfield players of his generation, was also a playboy and the move to Highbury proved a disaster. He was to become one of the great wasted talents alongside George Best, Peter Osgood, Stan Bowles, all mavericks with a taste for the high life. There was no end to the coming and goings. Old favourite John Radford went to West Ham for £80,000, the troublesome Peter Storey was suspended for refusing to train and play in the reserves. He moved on to Fulham where Campbell had taken over as manager but the hard man of the Double team soon drifted out of the game altogether. One man upset not to be going anywhere was George Armstrong. He had been promised a free transfer by Christmas. Goalkeeper Jimmy Rimmer also clashed with the manager and demanded a transfer, so too did Brady. But gates were up and the team were playing attractive football. Bolstered by the arrival of big Willie Young from Spurs in March, the team steadied itself at the back after a run of six successive defeats to finish a creditable eighth behind champions Liverpool. Love him or hate him Neill was putting Arsenal on the road to success again.

Controversy dogged Neill and the team throughout the summer and a tour to the far East and Australia, unpopular with the players before it started, saw Hudson and Macdonald sent home prematurely. They had been disciplined for drinking and setting a bad example to younger players. When they got home they were suspended and transfer listed. It was a godsend at this time that Don Howe was able to return to the club as Neill's right hand man and coach. Dave Sexton had been the favourite for the job but when he took over at Old Trafford, Howe did not need to be asked twice to leave Leeds and return to Highbury. Neill, who continually upset the players with his public criticism, now had the perfect buffer, and the team were able to settle down to a genuine bid for trophies again.

The team rebuilding was not complete. Rimmer moved up to Aston Villa and

We've done it! Pat Rice holds the Cup aloft in 1979.

Neill, with the help of chairman Denis Hill Wood, made one of his most astute signings by bringing Northern Ireland goalkeeper Pat Jennings from White Hart Lane for a paltry £40,000. Spurs let him go after 13 years because they felt they had a worthy successor in Barry Daines. But he never made it at the top level while Jennings was to play for the Gunners with distinction and a record 110 caps for his country until his 40th year.

With new striker Alan Sunderland from Wolves, Arsenal featured strong in the title race but were denied a place in the League Cup final by a Ray Kennedy goal for Liverpool and made it to Wembley in the FA Cup to meet Ipswich on a scorching May afternoon. But with Brady not fully fit, Arsenal disappointed and Ipswich, managed by Bobby Robson, made the day their own with a 77th minute winner from Roger Osborne. But Neill said his team would be back and the following May they were as good as his word with one of the Ipswich men in their ranks. Hudson had eventually been sold for £200,000 to Seattle Sounders and Neill quickly spent more than double that on Brian Talbot, a tireless worker in the engine room of midfield who also had a taste for scoring important goals.

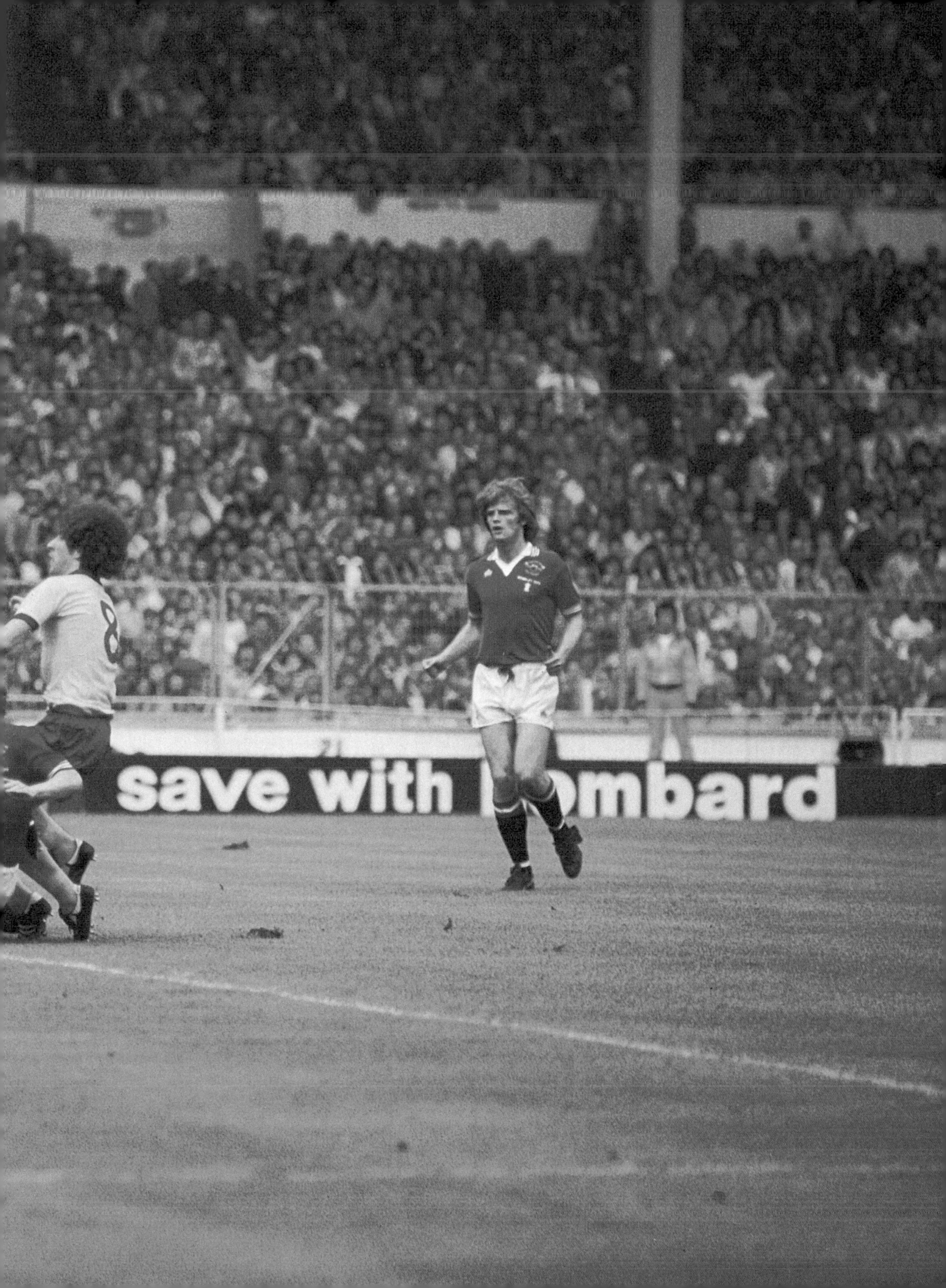
save with

Brady, Stapleton and Sunderland were at the peak of their careers with the Gunners and they brought the Cup back to Highbury for the fifth time with a dramatic victory over Manchester United. They led at half time with goals from Talbot and Stapleton but with the Cup apparently won, Gordon McQueen pulled a goal back and then Sammy McIlroy equalised. Brady then released Graham Rix down the left and his cross was met at the far post by the incoming Sunderland for one of Wembley's most memorable winning goals.

During the next season, this exciting Arsenal side was beginning to be compared with the Double team and they were to go one better by reaching two cup finals. But they had to take consolation in their two semi-final performances because this was a season that was to end in heartbreak. Brady, by this time regarded as one of the best left footed midfield players in the world, confirmed he wanted to improve his footballing education abroad but Arsenal fans were still treated to some magical performances as he guided the team towards a third successive FA Cup final and the Cup winners Cup final. Their major obstacle to a night of glory in Brussels proved to be Juventus. In an eventful first leg of the semi-final at Highbury Juventus took the lead through a twice taken penalty. David O'Leary was put out of the game by a tackle from Roberto Bettega, Italy's World Cup striker, and Marco Tardelli was sent off for a foul on Brady. Justice

Kenny Sansom, who has become one of the best defenders ever to play in the Arsenal colours.

was done when Bettega gave Arsenal their equaliser with an own goal.

Three days later they drew 0–0 with Liverpool in their FA Cup semi-final. A week later Arsenal produced one of the outstanding results in European competitive history by winning in Turin. Paul Vaessen, a professional for less than a year, scored the winner with two minutes left as Arsenal became the first British club to triumph there. The Italian club had not lost for ten years at home in Europe either. Five days later Sunderland scored after 20 seconds in the second replay with Liverpool but Dalglish made another game necessary with an injury time equaliser. Three days later at Coventry Brian Talbot's goal finally killed off Liverpool to book a Wembley date with West Ham. The four matches had been watched by 179,163 fans, paying £620,037.

Two days later Liverpool clinched the title again by beating Aston Villa 4–1 but Arsenal's nine free days before Wembley, however welcome, were not to give them the edge they needed against West Ham, who were a second division club at the time. Trevor Brooking deflected the ball past Jennings for an unusual winning goal and Arsenal never came to terms with West Ham's withdrawn centre forward Stuart Pearson. The omens were not good for the Cup-winners final against Valencia and with the score sheet blank after extra time it was to be decided on penalties. Mario Kempes, the Argentine World Cup star, and Brady missed the first attempts but everyone else scored to make it 4–4. Arias made it 5–4 for Valencia but Rix's shot was saved to produce a shattering climax for Arsenal.

Arsenal came home drained but there was still a UEFA Cup place in the offing if they could take four points from two games. Wolves were beaten 2–1 but in their 70th match of the season they ran out of steam and lost 5–0 at Middlesbrough. It is fair to say that Arsenal have never been quite the same since. Brady did as he said and moved abroad, ironically to Italy and Juventus. Graham Rix, dogged by injury, has never been able to fill his boots in midfield. Within a year, Frank Stapleton, by now the most coveted centre forward in Britain, had moved to Manchester United in acrimonious circumstances. Arsenal valued him at £2 million, United offered £750,000 and an independent tribunal disgusted Arsenal by settling on a fee of £900,000. Chairman Denis Hill-Wood was a major critic of the inflated transfer market but eventually he conceded that if you cannot beat them you must join them and the club were involved in the amazing Clive Allen transfer saga. The 19-year-old striker had scored 30 goals for QPR and the Gunners paid £1 million for him in the summer of 1980. Before the season opened he had gone to Crystal Palace in a package deal that took him and goal keeper Paul Barron to Selhurst Park and full-back Kenny Sansom to Highbury. Sansom has proved one of Neill's best buys, having become a fixture in the England team, but elsewhere the manager's forays into the transfer market began to produce more misses than hits and some of the new players he did buy turned out to be duds.

There was the unsuccessful experiment with Yugoslav World Cup captain Vladimir Petrovic who lasted just half a season in the hurly burly of the Football League, and £500,000 spent on centre forward Lee Chapman who never made the grade. Apart from the odd exception like Stewart Robson, a hard, grafting midfield player who could play for England one day, there have been few diamonds to come through the ranks. Neill's career as Arsenal manager was to founder in 1983 after one of his most spectacular coups in the transfer market. This was when he persuaded the young Scot Charlie Nicholas to sign in the face of opposition from Liverpool and Manchester United. Nicholas, then only 21, had scored 50 goals for Celtic and a wonderful goal for Scotland on his debut. He was then the best prospect to come out of Scotland since Kenny Dalglish – but, with the benefit of hindsight, clearly not equipped to restore Arsenal's fortunes single handed. Neill paid the price with the sack, and his successor, Don Howe, has been finding that the job is easier said than done.

Charlie Nicholas... it was soon clear he couldn't inspire the team all on his own.

Highbury Hall of Fame

George Armstrong

Geordie Armstrong was one of the great contributors to the Highbury cause. Arsenal snapped up the little left winger from Hebburn in the north east in 1961 and he went on to make a record 500 appearances until he moved on in the autumn of his career to Leicester in 1977. A specialist corner kicker, he had boundless energy and was a constant thorn in any defence except his own, where he was always helping out if needed. Geordie reached the peak of his career in the Double year after being a member of the Fairs Cup-winning side that beat Anderlecht. The biggest surprise of his career was that after winning England Under 23 caps he was never picked at senior level by Sir Alf Ramsey or Don Revie, although this of course was an era when wingers went out of fashion.

Joe Baker

Joe Baker's scoring record of 93 goals in 144 League games for the Gunners stands comparison with the best strikers. Though he was at Highbury during the one decade since the Twenties when the club failed to win a major honour, England international Baker was one of the few success stories of the time. Bought from Italian club Torino for a club record fee of £70,000 in 1962, Baker was top or joint top scorer in each of his four seasons at Highbury, striking up a partnership with Geoff Strong which netted a combined total of 52 goals in the 1964-65 season. He won eight England caps.

Alan Ball

The flame-haired little midfield terrier already had a glittering career behind him when Bertie Mee bought him for £220,000 from Everton to hold the side together in the disappointing aftermath of the Double win. Ball, who was to become a master of the short passing game, started at Blackpool and after being a member of England's 1966 World Cup-winning side at 19, moved to Everton two months later for £110,000. There, he became part of the famous Ball-Harvey-Kendall midfield which was at the heart of Everton's 1970 championship win. His arrival at Highbury arrested an alarming slide but for all his inspiration and enthusiasm he was destined not to win anything in teams which did not carry enough experience. He moved on to Southampton in 1976 where he became an invaluable influence for manager Lawrie McMenemy and has since gone into management.

Walley Barnes

Walley Barnes was a wartime discovery whose courage and determination twice helped him become one of Arsenal's most famous full-backs. The stylish, Brecon-born Barnes was an amateur with Portsmouth before joining the Gunners to play an important role in reviving the club's flagging fortunes when League action began again in 1946. His ability to play equally effectively with either foot meant he was at home in both full-back positions. He formed firm partnerships with both Laurie Scott and Lionel Smith and won 22 caps for Wales as well as a League championship and FA Cup-winner's medal. He made a total of 267 League appearances, battling back again after the second of his knee injuries reduced Arsenal to 10 men in the 1952 FA Cup Final and put him out of the game for 18 months.

Cliff Bastin

Cliff Bastin was still only 17 when Herbert Chapman made a trip to Exeter to sign him for Arsenal. The young Bastin was unimpressed by Chapman's overtures – soccer's maximum wage meant he could earn no more in London than he could playing for Exeter – and he agreed only reluctantly. He started at inside left but made his mark on the left wing where his speed and devastating left foot made him the most prolific goalscorer winger of his day. Bastin went on to become one of the Chapman immortals in an Arsenal forward line which earned a reputation as the greatest in the world. Apart from sharing in all the glories of the 30s, he also set a club scoring record of 150 goals in 350 league appearances between 1930 and 1947 and won 21 caps for England. He retired to return to his native Devon.

Liam Brady

When Liam Brady went to play in Italy in 1980 he left such a yawning gap in the Arsenal side that the club have never really found a successful replacement. The thousands of Highbury fans who took the little Irishman to their hearts dream constantly that he will return like the prodigal son and make the team tick again with that sweet left foot. They soon recognised that here was someone special when he broke into the team in 1973 and within a couple of seasons had established himself as a midfield general capable of leading the team to honours. Brady, a Republic of Ireland schoolboy international, was born in Dublin and joined Arsenal as an apprentice. Together with David O'Leary and Frank Stapleton he was among a trio of juniors who were to reach the very top of their profession and take Arsenal to three successive FA Cup Finals. He played a vital part

Cliff Bastin, the most prolific goalscorer of his day.

Liam Brady, the midfield dynamo who swept Arsenal to three successive F.A. Cup finals.

Opposite Top *George Armstrong – A record 500 appearances.* **Centre** *Joe Baker – 93 goals in 144 League games.* **Bottom** *Walley Barnes – Effective at right or left back.*

Preceding pages *Alex James shoots from the penalty spot against Blackpool in 1932.*

101

in the one Arsenal won in 1979 against Manchester United but he was desperately disappointed the next season when Arsenal not only lost the FA Cup Final to West Ham but were beaten on penalties by Valencia in the European Cup-winners' Cup. He had made no secret of his desire to play abroad and that summer Juventus paid £600,000 for his services to bring to an end a Highbury career of 235 League appearances and 43 goals. Since then he has enhanced his world class reputation with Sampdoria and Inter Milan while winning 50 caps and becoming captain of his country.

Charlie Buchan

Charlie Buchan was the son of an Aberdonian blacksmith and was born in London after his father came south to work at the old Woolwich Arsenal. He made only 102 League appearances while at Highbury but they must count among the most important in the club's history. He was already a major England star at Sunderland when Herbert Chapman signed him in 1925 and appointed him Arsenal captain. In three seasons Buchan helped to revolutionise not only Arsenal's style but the style of soccer in general through the adoption of the third back system. He was a lean, rangy six-footer whose ungainly style belied a remarkable sense of timing. He was an inspirational leader and a prolific scorer at either inside or centre forward. His £100-a-goal transfer from Sunderland is among soccer's most famous transactions. He scored a total of 49 in the League with Arsenal at an average of one every other game, including 19 in his first season when he was already 34 years old. In his long and varied career, he was also a schoolmaster, a soldier and a journalist but he will be remembered at Highbury as a great player and captain.

Charlie Buchan in action against Spurs in 1927.

Leslie Compton

Big Leslie Compton stands high in the Highbury roll of honour, a giant of a man whose 20 years at Highbury spanned two of the greatest periods in the club's history. His first-team appearances were limited to just 67 in the eight seasons before the war but the versatile Compton, who filled just about every position on the field during his career, returned afterwards to claim his first team place as a centre half and reap the rewards of his effort. He made 186 post-War League appearances, winning a championship medal in 1948 and a Cup-winners' medal in 1950, which was also the year he won long overdue England honours at the ripe old age of 38. He thus became the oldest player to make his England debut. Like brother Denis he was also a Middlesex cricketer. He died in 1984, aged 72.

Wilf Copping

The wing half partnership of Copping and Crayston is rated by many fans as the best Arsenal ever had, better even than Mercer and Forbes. The pair arrived in mid-1934 with Copping already an established England international with Leeds when George Allison moved in for him. He was a dour, temperamental former Yorkshire miner with enough superstitions to cover the whole team. He never shaved on match days, always put his left boot on first and insisted on being sixth man out. He was a ferocious tackler who fully lived up to his iron man image. One of his best performances was when he played for England against Italy as one of the Highbury seven. Copping played 166 League games for Arsenal between 1934 and 1939 and won two championship and one Cup-winner's medal. He made 20 England appearances and was eventually transferred back to Leeds.

Jack Crayston

Gentleman Jack was one of Arsenal's finest wing halves. He was the second signing of manager George Allison in 1934 and struck up an immediate rapport with fellow newcomer and wing half Wilf Copping. Crayston was born in Grange over Sands, Lancashire, and played for Bradford Park Avenue before his £4,000 move south. This was another of Arsenal's hire purchase arrangements, since Crayston was thought to have brittle legs and Bradford were to receive further payments of £250 a time as the player showed his fitness. In fact Crayston proved to be not only injury-free but one of the fittest men in soccer and Bradford received another £1,250. Like Copping, Crayston played for England as well as picking up two championship medals and a Cup-winner's medal in Arsenal's golden era. He was a tall, elegant player, fast, good in the air and a strong tackler. With the help of his long arms, he also became a pioneer of the long throw-in. He made a total of 168 League appearances before becoming Tom Whittaker's assistant and finally club manager in 1956.

Copping and Crayston – Rated by many as the best wing half partnership Arsenal ever had.

Ted Drake

Ted Drake was unquestionably Arsenal's greatest centre forward. He cost £6,000 from Southampton in March, 1934, a few months after Herbert Chapman's death, and immediately confirmed his worth with his lion-hearted courage and a glut of goals. His 42 in 1934-35 is still a club record (it included seven hat-tricks) and the following season he equalled the First Division individual record with all seven in the 7–1 win over Aston Villa. By the time he retired in 1945 he'd won

two championship medals, one FA Cup winner's medal (which he'd earned by scoring the winning goal against Sheffield United in 1936) and five England caps. His injuries bore testimony to his bravery in the goalmouth: during his career he sustained a hernia, a broken wrist, a gashed forehead and a series of cartilage injuries. He went on to successful management and led Chelsea to the League title in 1955.

George Eastham

George Eastham was more than a marvellously gifted footballer. He was a freedom fighter who changed the face of soccer in the Sixties. It was his one-man strike at Newcastle which won players the right to own their own contracts and became a 'cause célèbre'. Arsenal manager George Swindin signed Eastham for £47,500 in 1960 and the Blackpool-born inside forward went on to make 207 League appearances and score 41 goals. Eastham was a frail-looking player but his ability to beat his man and lay off the perfectly weighted pass made him one of the sweetest players of the day. He won 19 England caps and left the Gunners in 1966 to join Stoke.

Alex Forbes

Older Gunners fans talk about 'the great Alex Forbes', and with good reason. The big, red-headed Scot made an immediate impact by scoring with his first kick for Arsenal in 1948 and never looked back. The former ice hockey player was a fierce-tackling 22 year-old wing half who caught Tom Whittaker's eye while on a scouting mission to Sheffield United. Arsenal paid £13,000 for his services and Forbes became an integral part of their post-war success. Whittaker initially played him as an attacking inside forward though he had already won the first of 14 Scotland caps as a wing half and partnered Joe Mercer in this position at Arsenal. He also played on Arsenal's right wing on occasions and made a total of 217 League appearances. He narrowly missed out on a championship medal in 1948 (playing 11 games) but won a Cup-winner's medal in 1950 and a championship medal in 1953.

Top *Ted Drake – Arsenal's greatest centre forward.*
Above *George Eastham – Changed the face of soccer.*

Charlie George

Charlie George, born just around the corner from Highbury in Holloway, was the player who fulfilled every young fan's dream by coming off the terraces to become a star in the team at the age of 19. George appeared to have everything, pace, unbelievable natural skill, a devastating shot, a masterly long pass. His Highbury teammates were often left speechless in training by his sheer virtuosity. Many opponents had that feeling too. Don Howe told him he could become the Di Stefano of Arsenal. So what went wrong after he had played a major part in the Fairs Cup triumph of 1970 and the Double win the following season? The Cockney Kid was of such independent spirit that Howe never knew what sort of performance Arsenal would get out of him and while at Highbury he always had a young head on his shoulders. George had his problems with injuries too, particularly his knees, and played only 133 League games for the Gunners in six seasons. He always felt that he was not paid enough in comparison with other Arsenal stars and he had been hankering for a move for some time when Derby paid £90,000 for him in 1976. It was there that he won his solitary England cap – a sad reflection on a great player who could have become a legend.

George Graham

He came from Chelsea in the early weeks of the 1966-67 season as one of Bertie Mee's first signings in exchange for Tommy Baldwin and £50,000. He quickly made his mark up front alongside John Radford, becoming a consistent scorer and finished his first full season as top scorer with 12. Next season it was up to 20 but he and Radford were not proving a perfect match of personalities and he dropped back into midfield. It was here he tapped his all-round talents and Graham went to Wembley on four occasions with Arsenal; there were runners-up medals in two League Cups and the thrill of the Fairs Cup win. But he reached the peak of his career in the Double year – as many of the players did – and his performances realised a lifelong ambition to play for Scotland. This he did with distinction in 12 internationals, including a memorable tournament in Brazil.

Eddie Hapgood, Arsenal and England captain of the thirties, who Chapman turned into one of the all-time great left backs.

Opposite Top *Cliff Holton – Developed into a lethal centre forward.* **Centre** *Joe Hulme – A free-scoring outside right.* **Bottom** *David Jack – A proven good scoring record.*

Eddie Hapgood

Only Kenny Sansom can lay claim to Eddie Hapgood's title as Arsenal's greatest left back. The former Bristol milkman brought grace, elegance and, some say, arrogance to the position he filled with such distinction throughout the Chapman era. Those that knew him insist it was confidence rather than arrogance but no matter, Hapgood was the greatest of his day. He made 393 League appearances, won five championship medals, two Cup-winner's medals and was both captain of Arsenal and England, for whom he won 30 caps. His mighty presence on the football field was in contrast to the pale-faced wisp of a boy he was when Chapman signed him from non-League Kettering in 1927. In his early games Hapgood used to be knocked unconscious whenever he headed the ball. It was Tom Whittaker who identified the problem and took Hapgood off his vegetarian diet and built him up on steaks. Hapgood became one of the few players capable of blotting out the great Stanley Matthews, rated the finest outside right of his day.

Cliff Holton

Hot-Shot Holton was a typical example of Tom Whittaker's ability to spot and develop raw talent. Holton was playing for Ishthmian League club Oxford City as a full-back when Whittaker signed him in 1947. It took Holton three years to break into the first team but when he did so it was as a centre forward. Holton's tall, powerful build and lethal shot in either foot made him ideally suited for the position. He played 198 League games for Arsenal and scored 83 goals, winning an FA Cup runners-up medal in 1952 and a League championship medal the following season. In the latter part of his career he switched to wing half where he captained the club before moving on to Watford; there he set a club scoring record of 42 goals in a season.

Joe Hulme

Joe Hulme was reputed to be the fastest footballer in the game. He was one of Herbert Chapman's first signings, joining from Blackburn in 1926 and eventually becoming the first of the famous five – Hulme, Jack, Drake, James and Bastin. A free-scoring outside right, Hulme was also an outstanding cricketer who played for Middlesex. He was a fine crosser of the ball and was able, like Bastin, to cut inside full-backs to take as well as make goals. He played 333 League games, winning League and Cup-winner's medals at Highbury before going on to make a fifth Cup Final appearance with Huddersfield whom he joined in 1938.

David Jack

When Charlie Buchan retired in 1928, Arsenal's manager, Herbert Chapman, sent out the word to his scouts to comb the country for a suitable replacement: an inside right with a proven goal-scoring record at the highest level. Only one man matched up to Chapman's requirements... 29-year-old England international David Jack, then with Bolton Wanderers. Chapman had to break the British League transfer record by paying £11,500 to get his man and Jack repaid the Arsenal manager's faith in him by becoming everything and more Chapman could have expected. He became part of the great Hulme, Jack, Lambert, Drake, James, Bastin forward line and his elegant ball play and superb dribbling and shooting enhanced the Highbury legend of the thirties. Jack made 181 League appearances with Arsenal and scored 111 goals – a record of the highest consistency. He added to his Bolton Cup-winner's medal of 1923 with a second in 1930, won three championship medals and made a total of nine England appearances.

Alex James

Alex James is probably the greatest player ever to have worn the red and white shirt. He was signed from Preston in 1929 for £9,000 after Chapman had seen him torment England the previous year while playing for Scotland's famous Blue Devils at Wembley. But whereas he scored 60 goals at Preston in four seasons, James was turned into a schemer at Highbury. The change almost proved a disaster. After some early flops, Chapman was forced to drop him and it took the glamour and the glory of the FA Cup to rekindle his confidence. James came back into the side to inspire the 1930 Cup run which climaxed in his scoring one of the winning goals in the final against Huddersfield. He never looked back. He made a total of 231 League appearances, won four championship medals and two FA Cup winner's medals.

Pat Jennings

The man with the frying pan hands surprised the football world with his move to Highbury in 1977. An even bigger surprise was that Spurs allowed one of the world's great post-war goalkeepers to join the old enemy. The quiet Ulsterman was first spotted by Watford but after 57 appearances moved on to Tottenham. During 13 years there he won an FA Cup winner's medal, two League Cup winner's medals and a UEFA Cup winner's medal. Believing his career to be over at 32, Spurs let him go to Arsenal for £45,000. He played more than 300 games for Arsenal, appeared in three FA Cup finals and extended his international career to a record 110 caps for Northern Ireland.

Bob John

Bob John was the greatest discovery of Leslie Knighton the Arsenal manager sacked to make way for Herbert Chapman. The hard-tackling wing half was playing for his local club Caerphilly and was expected to join Cardiff City when Arsenal swooped in 1923 for one of their most famous transfer coups. John was actually signed in a hotel owned by the Cardiff chairman who was in an adjacent room discussing his own club's interest in the player as Knighton was secretly concluding the transfer. The Cardiff chairman was dumbfounded when he discovered what had happened. John became one of Arsenal's finest servants, playing in the famous Chapman sides and setting a club record of 421 League appearances (since passed by George Armstrong). John won three championship medals, one Cup-winner's medal and made 15 appearances for Wales. He retired in 1938 to become a coach at West Ham.

Jack Kelsey

Jack Kelsey was rightly regarded as the finest goalkeeper of his day and ranks among Arsenal's top three along with George Swindin and Pat Jennings. Kelsey was the village blacksmith at Llansamlet, Swansea, and playing for the local side Winch Wen when Tom Whittaker signed him in 1949. He was bought to understudy Swindin and succeeded him in 1951, going on to give Arsenal a decade of first class service. He made a total of 327 League appearances, won a League championship medal in 1953 and gained the first of his 41 caps for Wales in 1954. One of his proudest moments was playing in the Welsh side which reached the quarter-finals of the World Cup in Sweden in 1958.

Ray Kennedy

Ray was spotted by Arsenal's northeast scout and it led to a glittering career studded with five League Championship medals, one FA Cup winner's medal, one League Cup winner's medal, two European Cup winner's medals, one UEFA Cup winner's medal and one Fairs Cup winner's medal. He first made his name as a strong and fearless striker when only 19, as Arsenal won the Fairs Cup in 1970. His goal in the away leg of the final against Anderlecht gave the Gunners great heart despite a 3–1 scoreline and they triumphantly clawed back the deficit

Alex James – Became the great schemer at Highbury.

Opposite
Pat Jennings, arguably the Gunners' greatest ever 'keeper clears from Liverpool's David Johnson.

*Ray Kennedy –
Formed a feared striking partnership with John Radford.*

at Highbury. In the Double year he struck up a feared partnership with John Radford and the most important of his 26 goals came at White Hart Lane when a late header made certain of the title. The likeable Geordie possibly suffered by winning so much at an early age and a new challenge appeared in 1974 when Bill Shankly took him to Anfield for £200,000 as his last signing before retiring. New manager Bob Paisley switched him to midfield and his career took off to even greater heights bringing him international recognition in the shape of 17 England caps.

Jimmy Logie – Adored for his dribbling skills.

Jimmy Logie

Jimmy Logie was hailed as Arsenal's post-war Alex James, a diminutive Scot with teasing ball skills who inspired the triumphs of Tom Whittaker's teams. Logie, in fact, signed for Arsenal just before the war from Lochare Welfare, near Edinburgh. He was a bricklayer by trade though his 5ft 4in, 9-stone frame hardly fitted the image. Like James he became a maker rather than taker of goals at Highbury and shared in the post-war success of two League championships and two Wembley finals including the 1950 Cup victory. Logie was not so robust as James and was never rated as good a passer of the ball. But his brilliant dribbling made him a great Highbury favourite and he played a total of 296 League games, scoring 68 goals.

Reg Lewis

Reg Lewis was an outstanding goal-scorer who didn't let the war years cheat him of the success his talents deserved. He was a Brixton schoolboy who was also on Surrey's books as a bright cricket prospect when Arsenal signed him. He scored on his League debut in 1938 and was hailed as a successor to Ted Drake before League soccer came to a temporary halt. Despite the seven-year break, Lewis came back to fulfil his early promise, winning League and FA Cup medals in 1948 and 1950. He scored 29 goals in 28 games in the 1946-47 season and totalled 103 in 154 League appearances. His greatest triumph was in the 1950 FA Cup Final when he came out of a spell of indifferent form to score both goals in the 2-0 win over Liverpool.

Below *Malcolm Macdonald – 191 goals in 269 League appearances.* **Bottom** *Bob McNab - A godsend in the Dressing room.*

Malcolm Macdonald

Supermac's transfer fee was probably Arsenal's most publicised since Charlie Buchan's £100-a-goal deal in the Twenties. Arsenal paid £333,333 to Newcastle for the bustling England centre forward and goalscoring idol of Tyneside. But he started out in soccer as a full-back with Tonbridge then signed for Fulham, who converted him to centre forward but allowed him to go to Luton a year later in 1969. His goalscoring was sensational for two seasons until Luton cashed in and persuaded Newcastle to pay a club record of £185,000. He played 14 times for England before he signed for Arsenal in 1976 but amazingly scored in only one game when he hit a record five against Cyprus. Macdonald endeared himself to the Highbury fans by scoring 29 goals in his first season then 26 in his second but within three years was forced out of the game at the age of 29 by a knee injury and went back to Fulham as manager. Macdonald never won a championship medal and was a three-time Wembley loser, twice with Newcastle, once with the Gunners, but his 191 goals in 269 League appearances (42 in 84 for Arsenal) are his remarkable legacy to the game.

Frank McLintock

Quite simply, Frank McLintock was one of Arsenal's best ever captains. Successfully converted by Don Howe from a shrewd attacking wing half to central defender in the season Arsenal won the Fairs Cup, the Scotland international became the inspirational skipper of the Double side. The honours didn't end there because he was also named Footballer of the Year and made an MBE. McLintock made his name with Leicester in the early Sixties and appeared in two losing FA Cup finals. Arsenal paid £80,000 for him in 1964 and he was to be a loser in two League Cup finals at Wembley before lifting the FA Cup in 1971. The switch at 29 from wing half to centre half successfully prolonged his career and he was heartbroken when Bertie Mee let him go in 1973. McLintock proved the manager wrong by joining QPR and taking them to within a hair's breadth of the title in 1976 and he played on until he was 37 before going back to Leicester as manager himself.

Bob McNab

Bertie Mee put one over the great Bill Shankly to secure the services of one of the most talented left backs in the country, a man who became one of the key members of the Double side. Arsenal stepped into transfer negotiations at Liverpool

in September, 1966 to persuade McNab to move south from his home-town club Huddersfield for £65,000, then a record fee for a British full back. McNab, whose optimistic character was a godsend in the dressing room as Mee launched the Arsenal revival, took over from the long-serving Billy McCullough and went on to play 278 League games in eight seasons at Highbury. He read the game beautifully, was an astute tackler and developed into an exciting overlapping full back. During the Double year he was a vital part of a back four which became the rock on which Arsenal built their magnificent success. McNab eventually lost his place to Sammy Nelson and finished his career at Wolves. He won four England caps in 1969.

George Male

George Male became one of Highbury's reluctant heroes for his role in 'The Team That Chapman Built'. He was a wing half when Chapman called him into his office and told him he wanted to switch him to full-back. Male protested, but to no avail. Chapman's persuasive words led Male to say later: 'I left convinced that not only could I play right back but that I'd be the best right back in the world.' The quiet, powerful East Londoner from West Ham with few frills or flourishes became the first half of the famous Male and Hapgood partnership.

George Male – The quiet, powerful East Londoner.

111

He joined from Isthmian League side Clapton and went on to win four championship medals and one Cup-winner's medal. He made a total of 285 League appearances, and like Hapgood captained both club and country. He won 19 England caps and was one of the Arsenal Seven who played against Italy. He gave one of his finest performances in the 1936 FA Cup Final win against Sheffield United.

Terry Neill

Terry Neill's long association with Arsenal began in 1959 when he joined them as a 17-year-old after being spotted playing for Bangor City. He made his debut the following season as a wing half but was later switched to centre half by manager Billy Wright. He made 241 League appearances for the Gunners, finally losing his place in the heart of the defence to Frank McLintock, who succeeded him as captain. This intelligent, witty man was a strong, uncompromising player who could be physical or skilful as the situation demanded. He made up for his lack of pace with sound positional sense. He was good enough to make his Northern Ireland debut at 18 against Italy and he kept his place for 12 years, winning 59 caps and doubling as player manager and captain in his later years. One of the most memorable moments of his career came in his 50th international when he scored the winning goal at Wembley in a rare Irish victory. Terry left Highbury to become player-manager at Hull and at 29 was the youngest boss in the League. His management career was eventually to lead him to Tottenham in 1974 and then to Highbury in 1976 to succeed Bertie Mee. His masterstroke was to bring back coach Don Howe from Leeds and their partnership guided Arsenal to their three successive FA Cup finals in 1978, 79 and 80 plus their near miss in the Cup-Winners' Cup in 1980 when they lost to Valencia on penalties. But even this favourite son of Highbury could not escape the usual fate of managers when things begin to go wrong and after seven years in charge he was sacked at the end of 1983. It was his first real setback in a 25-year career in football.

Terry Neill – Guided Arsenal to three successive FA Cup Finals.

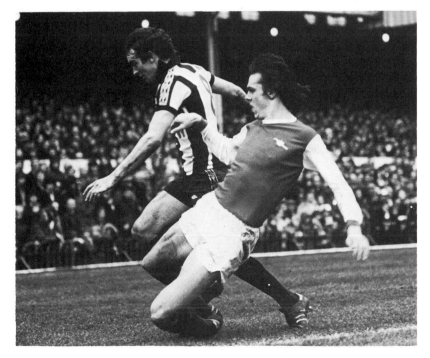

David O'Leary, a tower of strength in the Arsenal defence, seen here against West Bromwich Albion in 1978.

Charlie Nicholas

What a coup it appeared to be when Terry Neill persuaded Charlie Nicholas that Highbury was the place for his talents when he decided to move south of the border in the summer of 1983. Nicholas, the best young striker produced by Scotland since Kenny Dalglish, had sent Celtic fans into raptures with his 50 goals that season and Scotland supporters were in heaven when he celebrated his international debut in March with a memorable goal. When he let it be known that at 21 he was ready for a bigger stage, top clubs from England and the Continent were queueing up for his £650,000 signature. It came down to a three-cornered fight between Liverpool, Arsenal and Manchester United and to many people's surprise Arsenal won. Nicholas perhaps the best natural talent at Highbury since Charlie George, could shoot and pass like a dream,and when he scored twice on his debut it looked as if Arsenal, having lit the blue touch paper, could retire. But Nicholas, dazzled by the bright lights of London, and struggling to make an impact in an average Arsenal team, fizzled and spluttered like a damp squib. New manager Don Howe dropped him back into midfield to play a more expansive role but as yet there have only been tantalising glimpses of the form which could make him a world class player.

David O'Leary

Arsenal owe a great debt to a man called Gordon Clark. The scout has spotted many a potential star. When Clark saw the leggy young O'Leary play it took him five minutes to know he would be a good player and that he ought to sign for Arsenal. O'Leary was impressed and happily followed fellow Dubliners Brady and Stapleton to Highbury, although he was so homesick the club used to send him back home for six weeks at a time. By the time he was 21, this tall, lean and elegant player had 150 games for Arsenal under his belt and 10 caps for the Republic of Ireland. His secret is that he is a footballer who became a centre half, having been an attacking midfield player as a schoolboy. When it was decided to move him back in defence, it didn't stop O'Leary coming forward! Under Terry Neill and Don Howe, O'Leary's career prospered in the successful side of the Seventies. There were three FA Cup Final appearances and the Cup-winners Cup final which followed.

John Radford

John Radford, the likeable down-to-earth Yorkshireman who became the experienced half of one of the best scoring double acts of post-war football, was also one of the best investments Arsenal ever made. All he cost Billy Wright as a 15-year-old in 1964 was a £10 signing-on fee and the train fare down to London from his home in the mining community of Hemsworth. Radford went on to play 375 League games and score 111 goals before he moved on at 29 to West Ham for £80,000 at the end of 1976. Twenty-one of those goals came in the Double year when in partnership with the young Ray Kennedy he terrorised first Division defences. It was a pairing he never thought would work because they were both big, brave strikers in the typical English mould. But somehow they gelled instinctively, taking pressure off each other at vital moments, and for a couple of seasons were the most effective pair in the country.

Charlie Nicholas – So far only tantalising glimpses.

Following pages *Stewart Robson, powerhouse of the modern midfield.*

John Radford, half of Arsenal's formidable strike force during the Double Season, leads the attack against Manchester United in 1973.

Pat Rice

Everyone remembers Charlie George as the Arsenal fan who grew up to play for the team. But so was Pat Rice, and whereas George never fulfilled his enormous potential, Rice, a determined, quick and agile full-back, exceeded even his own expectations in a fabulous career at Highbury spanning 18 years from 1964 to 1982. He had already won international honours for Northern Ireland before he became a first team regular just prior to the Double year and the Liverpool final was to be the first of a record-breaking five FA Cup final appearances. Against Manchester United in 1979, he proudly lifted the Cup as captain, a role in which he excelled after succeeding Alan Ball in 1977. By this time he was also leading his country and he won the last of his 49 caps against England in 1980. Yet Rice, the Belfast boy who had come to England with his family at the age of ten to live only a kick away from Highbury, never thought he was good enough to make a career in the professional game. But manager Billy Wright and especially Don Howe recognised a never-say-die attitude which could help a shy young man overcome his deficiencies and Rice is the perfect example of a player whose enthusiasm and determination brought him out on top of more gifted players. When he gained experience, his strength and speed made him a match for any winger. He was later to lead by great example and after 397 League appearances and at the age of 33, Rice was granted a free transfer and Watford manager Graham Taylor snapped him up to lead Watford into the First Division.

Graham Rix

Graham Rix has not only been plagued by injuries during his career but had the unenviable job of trying to replace Liam Brady on the left side of midfield when the Irishman went to Italy. Born in Doncaster, Rix was an Arsenal apprentice and made his debut two years after turning professional with a goal against Leicester in 1977. He appeared in Arsenal's three successive FA Cup Finals and then suffered probably the worst moment of his career when his missed penalty cost the Gunners the European Cup winners Cup against Valencia in 1980. It did not stop the new Arsenal skipper making progress towards the England team and the first of his 17 caps came against Norway in the World Cup qualifiers. He was an important member of Greenwood's team in the finals in Spain. Rix played against France, Czechoslovakia, Kuwait, West Germany and Spain. But with another World Cup coming up in Mexico, Rix was hit hard by injury again in 1984–85, a season in which Arsenal could have done with his influence.

Herbie Roberts

The gunsmith's apprentice from Oswestry was Arsenal's most famous pre-war centre half. He was among the new breed who stayed back as a 'stopper' instead of foraging up with the forwards, and with his tall physique and mop of red hair, he stood out like a lighthouse in the Arsenal defence. Roberts was nicknamed 'the Policeman' because he was always on a beat around the penalty area. Arsenal signed him in 1926 on the recommendation of the local Highbury milkman, who was a distant relative. But Roberts didn't make his first team mark until he took over from Jack Butler shortly after Chapman adopted his third back formation at the end of the decade. He made 297 League appearances during the golden era and only once blotted his copybook – when he scored two own goals in two minutes against Derby.

Kenny Sansom

Kenny Sansom is a fixture at left back for Arsenal and England and he's such a consistently good performer that, barring serious injury, he should become the first Arsenal player to win 100 caps for his country. His international potential had already been spotted and before Kenny made an impressive full England debut against Wales that year he had been capped at schools, youth and Under 21 level. It was a year later that he moved to Highbury and by now football was into the era of the £1 million transfer. Kenny moved in a swap valued at £1.3 million which took striker Clive Allen and goalkeeper Paul Barron to Palace. Kenny quickly became a Highbury favourite, has become a cornerstone of the Arsenal defence in more than 200 League appearances, and rates as one of their best-ever left backs.

Peter Simpson

If Radford and Kennedy were the battering rams that broke down every door in their path, Simpson and McLintock were the twin padlocks on Arsenal's mean defence which conceded only 29 goals in the Double year. Yet Simpson, who spent his whole career at Highbury and was very much the quiet man of the side, missed the first 17 games after a cartilage operation. When he returned against Ipswich, he became an ever present and silenced the critics who said he was not good enough for Arsenal. Simpson set himself such high standards that he was never satisfied with his play but his teammates recognised him as the great unflappable at sweeper, always neat and tidy in his play, a hard tackler and the master of playing football out of tight situations with that lovely touch in his left foot. A slow starter after being an apprentice, Simpson established himself in 1967-68. He played in the two losing League Cup final teams, the Fairs Cup-winning side, the Double success and then the FA Cup Final defeat by Leeds a year later. He made 353 League appearances for the Gunners, scoring ten goals and

Following pages Kenny Sansom, who came to Highbury in a £1 million swap for Clive Allen.

played his last game in the First Division in January 1978. Sir Alf Ramsey picked him in his original 40 for the 1970 World Cup but he never made it to Mexico or the England team.

Frank Stapleton

When Frank Stapleton left Arsenal for Manchester United in the summer of 1981 – a bitter blow to all at Highbury – United, in many eyes, were getting the best all round centre forward in Britain. Arsenal put a £2 million price on the Irishman who was averaging 23 goals a season for them. United offered a derisory £700,000 and they still only paid a bargain £900,000 after an independent tribunal was called upon to settle a furious dispute. Stapleton, a shy man off the field, did all his talking on it in terms of world class performances and memorable goals. In his early years at Highbury he showed great natural heading ability and a brave attitude which denied the existence of lost causes. Bertie Mee had doubts about his pace and control but Stapleton was willing to work hard and in partnership with first, Malcolm Macdonald, and then the skilful Alan Sunderland, he matured into a great centre forward, a fixture for Arsenal and the Republic of Ireland. One of his great attributes was patience; centre halves would think they had played him out of a game only for Frank to take the one chance that came his way. Stapleton was one of three famous Dubliners in the side at the same time, together with Liam Brady and David O'Leary. Like Bradey, after nine years and four Cup Finals, he felt he needed a fresh challenge and United were the lucky ones to provide it for him.

Peter Storey

There have been few hard men in post-war football to compare with Peter Storey, whose gifts as a footballer were so often clouded by the controversies which marred his career on and off the field. What cannot be denied is that Storey, when he moved into midfield from defence in the injury crisis which launched the Double year, became the vital ballwinner Arsenal needed. He lived more than died by the sword and his fearless approach in a tough, uncompromising era of football was to win him 19 England caps under Sir Alf Ramsey. His short-fused temper let him down on many occasions and led to a series of sendings-off during his 16 years and 387 League games at Arsenal, whom he joined as a 15-year-old schoolboy. The final brush with authority came in 1977 when this son of an exiled Geordie miner walked out on the club when, after being at the top for so long, he found that he couldn't face another game in the reserves. Manager Terry Neill put him on the transfer list and a month later he moved into the second division with Fulham, where he played only 17 games before drifting sadly out of the game.

Top *Peter Simpson – Unflappable in the tightest situations.* **Above** *Peter Storey – A fearless approach to the game.*

Alan Sunderland

Arsenal fans will have one vivid memory of Alan Sunderland as he wheeled away in triumph after scoring the last-minute winner against Manchester United in the 1979 FA Cup Final at Wembley. With Arsenal apparently coasting to a 2-0 victory the match suddenly exploded into life in the last five minutes when Gordon McQueen and Sammy McIlroy goals pulled United level. But just when extra time seemed certain, Liam Brady found Graham Rix and his cross eluded everybody except hit-man Sunderland who slid in the winner at the far post. Sunderland's pace and finishing made his name at Wolves and when he moved to Highbury in 1977 for £450,000 he quickly struck up a successful partnership with Frank Stapleton. His most productive season followed that FA Cup triumph when he netted 24 goals and won his one England cap. Arsenal's decision to bring back Tony Woodcock from his two-year exile at Cologne spelt the end for Alan's first team place and Ipswich were quite happy to snap him up in 1984.

Below *George Swindin – An inspirational goalkeeper*
Bottom*Brian Talbot – More than a non-stop runner.*

George Swindin

Tom Whittaker rated George Swindin as the finest goalkeeper Arsenal ever had. He was signed from Bradford City a couple of weeks before the 1935 FA Cup Final and made his debut at the start of the following season, replacing Alec Wilson. An inspirational goalkeeper, brave, agile and perceptive, Swindin played 271 League games in an 18-year Highbury career broken by the war. He won his first championship medal in 1938, his second in 1948 and qualified for his third with 14 games in his farewell season in 1953. One of his most memorable performances was in the 1950 Cup Final against Liverpool when his scarlet jersey and marvellous saves made it another red-letter day for the Gunners. After retiring Swindin stayed on at Highbury and succeeded Jack Crayston as manager in 1960.

Brian Talbot

Arsenal paid a club record £450,000 for the Ipswich and England midfield dynamo in January, 1979. Four months later, Talbot, at 26 achieved the unique distinction of winning FA Cup winner's medals with different clubs in successive seasons. In 1978 he was in the Ipswich side who beat Arsenal 1–0 and then played in Arsenal's 3–2 win over Manchester United. The following season he made it a hat-trick of Wembley Cup Final appearances but this time was on the losing side when West Ham won an all-London battle 1–0. Another big final followed when the Gunners lost the European Cup-winners Cup on penalties to Valencia, but Talbot's non-stop running and vital goals have made him one of the club's best signings of recent seasons. He has six England caps.

Bob Wilson

Bob Wilson, as brave a goalkeeper as any to play for Arsenal, was an unlikely star and his story is one of the most unusual to come out of the famous Double side. A son of Chesterfield, which has produced many famous goalkeepers, Wilson originally planned to be a teacher and played for Wolves as an amateur. He refused to turn professional because he dreamed of playing for the British Olympic team. He drifted away from Molineux and joined Arsenal, still as an amateur, in 1963 and played five times in the First Division before turning professional a year later. There was a major row when Wolves heard of it and the League stepped in to decide Wolves should receive a £5,500 transfer fee. Wilson turned out to be a late developer and eventually won the battle for goalkeeper's jersey from Geoff Barnett in the season 1968-69 when he picked up a League Cup loser's tankard after the shock defeat by Swindon. But after that it was success all the way in the Fairs Cup and the Double year plus two Scotland caps. Bob retired in 1974 to become one of Britain's best known commentators.

Index

Photographic Acknowledgements

Cover photographs by Peter Robinson
& All Sport/Trevor Jones

All colour photographs by Peter Robinson

Black and white photographs supplied by:
Syndication International and STW Picture Library
While every effort has been made, in some cases
it has not been possible to trace the copyright
owners of certain photographs and STW Picture
Library invite such individuals or companies
to contact them via the publishers.